Love
Leaves
No
Regrets

*An Insightful View of
Displaced Children Through
the Eyes of a Former Foster Child*

Robert E. Colwell

Duncan & Duncan, Inc., _Publishers_

For information, review copies or book order inquiries, contact Duncan & Duncan, Inc., 2809 Pulaski Highway, P.O. Box 1137, Edgewood, Md 21040. Telephone: 410-538-5579.

Library of Congress Catalog Card Number: 96-83028

Colwell, Robert E.
  Love Leaves No Regrets
    1. Foster care 2. Child Welfare 3. Parenting 4. Orphanage 5. Foster homes 6. Foster parents 7. Foster children 8. Sociology, foster care treatment and the foster care system 9. Foster care system, the administration of 10. Children, treatment of

Biblical passages shown in this book are from the King James version of the Bible, except where otherwise noted.

ISBN: 1-878647-28-8

10-9-8-7-6-5-4-3-2-1

Dedication

This book is dedicated to all the geniuses who society either mistakenly rejected or was unable to recognize; and to those who untiringly forged ahead, though a wedge was placed between them and their dreams.

Acknowledgments

The following people have directly or indirectly helped
to make this book possible:

Bronwyn Beavers
Darrell Bush
Sandra Chase
Betty Colwell
Doris Colwell
Patricia Dawson
Dr. Edwin Derensbourg
Gary Hogans
Sharon Johns (Deceased)
Dr. Elliot Mason
Bob Mecado
Zena Oglesby

Regi Pope
Victoria Rabb
Karen Skiba
Woodsie Tidwell
Jennifer Ramsey-Wallace
Celestine Ware
Joe Westmoreland
Cynthia Willard

and most of all, my wife, Angela; my sons, Ryan and Justin; my stepson, Aaron; and, my daughter, Chelsea.

Contents

Foreword

*A*s Executive Director of the Institute for Black Parenting, a nationally known Adoption and Foster Family Agency, I get many calls for interviews. One day in 1993, my public relations staff scheduled me for an interview with a religious radio station in the Los Angeles, California area. The name of the program was *Love and Order* and the interviewer was Reverend Robert Colwell. We could not envision that this interview would result in Reverend Colwell writing a book and traveling around the nation providing training that could conceivably alter the Child Welfare system in this country.

The interview began, as they often do, with the interviewer being stunned by the actual numbers of children in the local foster care system (at the time it was 45,000 children in the immediate area). However, there was something different about his reactions. He was riveted by the data. He had more than a passing interest in the numbers and the plight of the children. I soon learned that Reverend Colwell was raised in the foster care system himself.

The interviewee became the interviewer. I asked questions and was amazed at his answers. I was fascinated by his journey through the foster care system. It was not a "success story" in the traditional sense. Even more surprising to me was his ability to frame his experiences in a way that allowed you to learn something profound and usable from them.

Several people have been able to tell their story of foster care in a tender and moving fashion, leaving you to make of it what you will. Reverend Colwell has an ability to step back and view his experiences with an eye toward what happened and why.

His style is confrontive and utterly "in your face." As he has admonished his listeners, "Don't judge me by my foster care status." He shows us that real interest makes us find out who these children really are—not a number in a case-load report—but real people with their own unique talents, abilities and potentials. The power of his message is matched only by the power of his personal appearance. He is deceptively quiet and unassuming. Yet when he begins to talk, an intensity so striking flashes bright enough to awaken even the most disinterested social worker and/or foster parent.

Reverend Colwell has the ability to frame his message in terms other than "look at me and feel sorry." He gives us the reasons why people become foster parents. He gives us insight into his transition from foster child to a reasoning adult who had to find the causes for what happened to him and his siblings. He searches successfully for meaning and he is kind enough to share it with us in ways that allow us to do more than feel sorry for him.

His message has meaning for all the players in this system we call Child Welfare. Social Service practitioners will receive solid instructional ways in which to view families and individuals who want to become foster parents. Administrators of these systems will be challenged to face the system they perpetuate.

Foster parents are challenged to search their souls for the genuine reasons for their desire to parent, and finally, and most importantly, foster children and adults raised in foster care will be able to make sense of the senseless. They can at least begin to understand that the system itself is so inept that it does not seem to matter who is in charge, how caring the staff or the level of caring of the foster parents themselves.

The following account of the Reverend Robert Colwell will no doubt take its rightful place at the forefront of the foster care/adoption reform movement. Not a movement to destroy the good with the bad, but hopefully one that will call for the massive changes that will help us prevent the emotional, psychological and often physical destruction of another generation of children.

Zena Oglesby, Jr.
Executive Director
The Institute for Black Parenting

Introduction

A few years ago, a foster mother called my office re-
questing counsel. She had accepted a seven-year-old
boy into her home who desperately needed a mother, and
she had since come to regret it. Having two biological
children (a nine-year-old daughter and a six-year-old son)
she was concerned that her foster child's presence was
having an adverse effect on them. She had heard of my
training for foster parents and wanted to know if I agreed
with her decision to relinquish him.

"Do you love him?" I asked.

"I'm trying to, but it's so hard to please him. I go
out of my way to make him happy; whatever I do for my
own kids I do for him. Yet, he's always getting angry and
I believe it's affecting my other children."

I explained how important it is that children be carefully matched with the proper foster family. A proper family is, first and foremost, one that is capable of loving them. I explained that additional consideration is necessary when placing a child, particularly one who has never been nurtured, with foster parents who have biological children of similar age.

"I treat all my kids the same," she insisted.

Perceiving the problem, I asked, "Does your six year old child ever jump up and down on your bed?"

She paused and before she could answer I continued, "And does your foster child?" By her silence, I knew I had hit home.

"Do you recover as quickly when angered by your foster child as when angered by your own? And if, when the children are playing and something is accidentally broken, is your facial expression the same regardless of which child is responsible? Children will judge you by your ability to be fair and impartial. Feeling less favored, foster children usually expect a more rapid and harsher response when the fault lies with them.

"Do you have less patience with one or the other in waiting for a response to your demands? Do you listen more intently to one than the other?

"Just as those who lose their eyesight seem to increase their sense of hearing, children who lose their biological parents are often more sensitive to acts of inequality. I would think that your foster son, in light of his background, would have particular difficulty comprehending and accepting a double standard."

The concern in her voice let me know that she really

did care for him and that she was, in fact, a good mother. "I've discussed this issue with a number of people," she said, "but you're the first person to ever raise the possibility that the problem could have something to do with me."

I then said, "If you think you can learn to love him, I suggest you give it a little more time. Once you learn to love him, that love will leave you with no regrets."

Too often, unhappiness is the result of simple misunderstandings.

After living in New York for eighteen years, I moved to Los Angeles. Eighteen years later, my brother, Raymond, unexpectedly appeared at my door. I was stunned to learn that he had been in Los Angeles for a week and had no intentions of looking me up. Only at the last minute did he decide to stop by on his way back to the airport.

He shared with me how he and my other two brothers were told by their foster mother that no one, including me and our sister, Betty, cared anything at all for them—and they believed her. The infrequency of our phone calls helped to fortify that belief. Consequently, in spite of mistreatment by their foster mother, they felt obligated to show gratitude that she alone would take them in.

The following year on Thanksgiving Day, all three of my brothers, Raymond, Maxie, and Freddie, came to Los Angeles to visit me and my family. Betty and my grandmother were already in Los Angeles. Doris, my younger sister, came down from Oakland. It was our first time being together since entering the foster care system, and it was my first time seeing Freddie in over twenty years. Many of the stories they shared about their foster care experiences were quite disturbing and they were overwhelmed by some of mine. I explained how God's love and truth had lifted me from the weight of my past, setting my spirit free. Their eyes sparkled as they reached to embrace the truth. For so long my brothers and sisters felt abused and abandoned, but it was clear by the conclusion of our visit that love had left them with no regrets.

Love Leaves No Regrets is a powerful truth that begs us to examine our relationships with those we say we love. It's a message that must be shared. I believe it is vividly represented in the contents of this book.

Robert E. Colwell

One

True Love

I was my mother's favorite child. No, she never said so, but there was something about the way she looked at me. Tommie, my mother, was eighteen-years-old when her first child was born. I was the second of her six children; however, we were the product of three different men, none of whom she was ever married to.

Her first lover was a big, strong, handsome man named Frank, whom my mother and several other women were crazy about. Unfortunately though for my mother, a baby was not in his immediate plans.

The second man, my father, though not very tall, was handsome and well-built. It was my mother's decision not to marry him, though she did love him. Injuries incurred during the Korean War caused him to turn to alcohol; and the difficulty of finding and maintaining work snuffed out any hope there may have been for the two of them.

The last four children were by the same man whose name was Freddie. He was clean-cut, well-dressed, well-built and had lust-filled eyes that never seemed to close. He was an older man and flattered to be involved with such a younger woman. A couple of nights a week, he would stay with us—whenever he could give his wife a good enough excuse for being out all night.

Predictably, before long she found out, particularly since she only lived at the other end of the street. Once in a while, she would come by our house late at night and yell for him to come out but he would never answer.

So often I would wonder: "Why does she put up with him? What could he possibly say to his wife to make her believe that he actually loves her?" Even at my young age I knew he couldn't possibly love her because her words had absolutely no impact on him. If someone truly loves you it will be easy for you to seize their attention and persuade them to meet your reasonable request or demand.

True love assures that maximum consideration is given to every decision involving your happiness, your future and your well-being. I can remember thinking to myself: "How is it that I can feel sorry for this man's wife, and even somewhat guilty and yet he does not feel anything?" I appropriately labeled him selfish and callous, even though with my mother and her children he showed only kindness, patience and respect. I swore I would never be like him.

My mother and I had a special relationship. We depended on one another and always were able to talk about anything. She had confidence in my ability to reason and showed respect for my opinions, even when I was only eight years old.

She was a talented violinist, bright, tenacious, and was recognized by city and school officials for her strong community leadership. Back-to-back babies made her life more difficult to control, nonetheless, she was determined to make the best of it and gain optimum advantage for her children. One of the most important lessons I learned from her was that true love always listens and always responds accordingly.

Love Listens

It was my second week in the fifth grade. I started the year with only one new outfit which I wore to school every day for the first week. My mother had promised me five new outfits but her welfare check only allowed her to get one.

"Wait til the first of the month and I promise I'll get you the other outfits," she said.

So when the first came, I left for school believing it to be my last day of embarrassment. When school was out I ran home excited, only to hear that she still wasn't able to get the other outfits, not even one. I was crushed! The thought of wearing that same outfit again, or an old one (now too small) was more than I could bear. The next day as I left for school, it seemed all I could do was get one foot to go in front of the other. At that pace the usual fifteen minute walk would have taken almost forty.

As I approached the end of the block I heard footsteps coming up behind me. A large arm draped my shoulder and a sobbing voice, unlike any I had ever heard before said, "I'm sorry, Robby. Please, please forgive me." I could see in her tears that it hurt her as much to disappoint me as it did for me to put those clothes back on.

"I was thinking you didn't care," I said.

"No, I would have done anything to get the clothes you wanted," she replied. Her words were like warm milk to a hungry baby. Instantly, I was transformed into Mommy's little man again.

"Thank you, Mommy," I said. "You can go back now, I'll be alright."

As I continued on toward school, I could see out of the corner of my eye that every few feet she would turn her head back to look at me. It was clear that she truly loved me and her ears were open to everything I had to say. Somehow, wearing that outfit didn't seem so painful anymore.

Dad

I was nine years old when my biological father died. Smitty, as his friends called him, was a kind, honest, and thoughtful man, well liked by all who knew him. Most would agree that the Korean War had had a devastating effect on him. Mentally and physically he was not the same man.

I only saw him six times and each meeting was by

coincidence. The only words I remember him saying to me were, "Next week I'm gonna buy you that new bike I promised you." Each time I would happen upon him, no matter how long it had been, he would assure me that he had not forgotten and, "would pick up the bike next week." I believed him: that is, I believed he had not forgotten me and that he very much wanted to get me a bike.

"Mommy," I asked hopefully, "is my daddy really going to buy me a bicycle?"

"He said he would," she answered. "I'm sure he's trying to."

After our third encounter I realized that the talk of the neighborhood was probably true; that the little money my father made was spent on alcohol which helped him forget his past and escape the future. By this time his words of promise had little effect on me. After the fourth meeting, I began to feel that had he spotted me walking towards him, he would have ducked out of sight to avoid having to explain anything. I felt sorry for him—and for me. I could tell he was embarrassed by my apparent loss of faith (he needed to know that I believed in him.) And to think, all I really wanted was to get close to my dad but the bike got in the way.

At age thirty-six, Smitty died due to complications from war related injuries. As I peered into his casket, I remember feeling sad that I did not know him well enough to cry. But when I think of him, I'm glad I can say that despite his flaws, his failure to buy me a bike and the fact that I never spent more than ten minutes at a time with him, the love seen in his eyes and the warmth of his smile was enough to leave me with no regrets.

Sudden Change

It was my mother's 31st birthday. Skipping down the street to Nick's Deli, I was thinking: "What a coincidence; my mother is in the hospital giving birth on her birthday." Actually, the baby wasn't due for another month, but complications caused her to go in early.

As I approached the store my best friend was coming out.

"Hey man, what's goin' on?" I said, cheerfully. His face looked like he had just been slapped.

"I don't want to make you cry," he replied, and he kept on walking.

What is he talking about, I wondered. I took two steps forward then halted suddenly as my mind shifted to Mach speed. "No way! No way!" I said to myself. I entered the store, and as I took a loaf of bread from the shelf I noticed that everyone was staring at me. And Nick's voice (which today was unusually tender) made it impossible to dismiss the signs which pointed toward one conclusion.

The journey home was like traveling down an empty freeway and finding all the exits closed. The woman who was taking care of us while my mother was in the hospital was standing in front of our apartment talking to my mother's best friend. Neither one would look at me. I went inside and stood at the window trying to read their lips. A few minutes later a car pulled up, and all the people inside were crying. I ran to the bedroom, grabbed my stuffed tiger, and diving onto my bed I swam in my tears to reality. When my heart finished struggling with the facts, I looked at my brothers and sister, ages two, three, five, seven, and thirteen and thought to myself, "What are we going to do without a mother?"

Shortly thereafter, a social worker came by to inform us that we would have to be placed in foster care. My mother was an only child, which left only my grandmother as a possible guardian. Gramma was fifty-seven years old, had never been married and still bore the scars of an unpleasant childhood—herself being raised in an orphanage and foster home. Because she was our grandmother the county would not offer her the same money to care for us as they would a foster parent. After striving all of her life just to make ends meet, the thought of quitting her job shortly before making pension to care for six grandchildren, and having no one else to rely on, was terrifying.

For two straight weeks following my mother's death, the only time I saw my grandmother without tears in her eyes was when a social worker was present. She resented the system and everyone who worked in it.

I tried to appear optimistic as they loaded us up to take us away. Some neighbors came to wish us well, others waved cautiously from across the street or from a window.

"Don't worry 'bout 'em, Miss Colwell, they'll be alright!," yelled Mrs. Williams from across the street.

The social worker politely said good-bye, but my grandmother gave no response. Briskly, she waved at us for a moment then stood motionless with her chin held high, trying hard to hide her helplessness. Instead of us leaving the city it seemed like the city was leaving us. Where are all of our friends, I wondered? Why must we live with strangers when our mother did more than any other woman to help this community?

My mother helped many of our neighbors' kids by starting the first Cub Scout troop in our area, which became the largest pack in the city. And while volunteering her time to sit on the Mayor's committee, she convinced the city to build a playground for the enjoyment of everyone in our community. I could not believe that in this great, big city, there was not one person who would take us in. I was soon stunned by the reality that apparently, even in the entire state no one was willing to accept us.

My eyes seemed to knock on every door we passed as we drove down the street. I wondered if they knew we were on our way to an orphanage.

Reality

66 **Y**our new home is not quite ready for you," explained the social worker, as we followed the wind-
ing road leading to the front of the orphanage. It was a
large complex located on the back wing of a hospital, in a
seemingly desolate area.

"**I**'m going to leave you here while **I** check on your
new home and **I**'ll be back soon to get you," she promised.

The Orphanage

We entered the front door with just the clothes on our
backs. After a friendly but formal greeting, we were led
by a nun down a number of long corridors for a tour and
brief orientation. The hard tile floors and hollow sound

of her voice echoing off the empty walls made it impossible to escape the reality that we were now living in an institution.

"Robert, this is where you will sleep," said the nun, as she opened the over-sized door to a large hospital-like room. The ceiling was high and the walls were mint green, with large classroom-type windows which required a six-foot pole in order to be opened. Hospital-like beds lined both sides of the room, each with a hardwood chair and night stand.

"I want my brothers to stay in here with me," I demanded, noticing that there were only two empty beds.

"Alright," she answered, agreeably. "I'll set them up at the far end of the room. Your sisters will be at the other end of the hall."

That first night was most difficult. I got very little sleep trying to comfort my three brothers, Maxie, Raymond and Freddie, ages two, three and five respectively, who cried off-and-on throughout the night, begging to sleep with me. How confused they must be, I thought. How insecure, knowing that the person they feel safest with is only eleven years old.

With heavy eyes I noticed that the stars were slowly beginning to disappear. Concern for my brothers caused my own pain and fears to fade. As the morning sun crept into the room and removed the shadows from the wall, I was finally able to fall asleep. We were awakened by the sound of the morning bell. I arose quickly and gathered my brothers, hoping that the social worker would come early.

"Place all pajamas in the laundry bag and get clean pants and shirts from the closet," instructed a young nun, as she tried to comfort a little boy who woke up crying for his mother. None of the kids seemed to be very happy there; most all of them had a nervous look, as if it were their first day at pre-school.

Soon, another bell sounded and we all lined up for breakfast. The menu read: hot chocolate, hot cereal and toast. It was that meal; the lumpy, lukewarm, tasteless cream of wheat cereal that made me miss my mother even more. The idea of sitting in a room eating with a lot of strange children, day after day, and then getting up and walking out with them into the next room where we slept, left me longing for privacy and the comfort of a real home.

After filling our stomachs with hot chocolate and toast, I silently prayed, "Lord, please get us out of here."

From that point on, my only memory of the orphanage is that of an incident involving a very cute, six or seven year-old girl. I can't recall what time of day it was, but I was standing in my usual spot, in front of the window, when I noticed five young boys huddled around a bed looking down at the floor. One by one they would take turns going under the bed. Assuming that they had stolen something, I went over and peeked under the bed, totally unprepared for what I would see.

A little girl was lying on her back with her dress pulled up to her neck and a boy was on top of her. She had long, blonde pigtails and big, green eyes which exuded the confidence of a seventeen year old. Her shameless smile frightened me. (I had never heard of a girl her age engaging in such an adult activity, and never heard of anyone having five partners.) It was indeed a very disturbing experience for me. I turned away quickly and went back to the window and stood there—and was still standing there eight days later when the social worker came and rescued us.

My Hero

It was a Friday morning, close to midday. I was tying my brother's shoe when the same nun who greeted us the first day we arrived came over to my bed and said, "Your social worker is here and you'll be leaving today." My heart leaped for joy.

"Are we going with her now?" I asked.

"Yes," she replied with a smile. "Follow me." Never was I more excited about seeing anyone.

"Let's go, guys," I said, motioning to my brothers. I ran over to say good-bye to Juan, the only friend I made the entire time I was there. It really hurt me to see the look on his face. It seemed he wanted to cry but had no more tears. "I'll ask my new foster parents if you can come too," I promised.

As we approached the front office and I saw the social worker, I felt as though I wanted to run to her. Although I can't remember her name, at that particular moment she was not only my hero (beating out Mighty Mouse and The Lone Ranger) but the most important person in my life as well. No one else knew as much about my past, present and future as she did. She knew all the members of my family, the disruption caused by the death of my mother, the lifestyle we were accustomed to and the pain we endured in the orphanage. She even knew things that I didn't know, such as where we were going and how long we would most likely be there.

"Why, hello there," she greeted us, happily. "Sorry I took so long. We had hoped to place all six of you children in the same home, but it didn't work out. So for now, we can at least place you four boys together and place your sisters together with another family."

"Where are we going?" I asked.

"You boys will be in the Bronx," she replied, "and your sisters will be going to White Plains."

"How far is White Plains from the Bronx?" I asked.

"About 30 to 40 miles," she stated. "But don't worry, we'll make sure you have many opportunities to visit." We waved good-bye to the staff and headed for the car.

The Guardian

After a long drive, we pulled in front of a large brown house. "Here we are, said the social worker.

It was an older-looking house with a large, fenced side-yard adorned with grapevines that extended nearly the entire length of the house. An elderly man looked up from his garden, waved and smiled warmly at us as we climbed the steps to the front door. Answering the doorbell was a nice looking woman in her late thirties who greeted us with a big smile and invited us in.

The moment I saw her face, I remembered how my mother would often compliment me on being very perceptive for a boy my age. Those words helped me to trust my conclusion that this new arrangement was not going to work. The woman's smile was plastic. Her presence was void of any domestic virtue and the look in her eyes did not match the message of her mouth. Actually, she acted as if we had caught her at a bad time. Once inside it seemed she was hoping that the social worker would hurry up and leave.

"We're so glad you were able to take all four boys," said the worker. "I know it means so much to them."

Had I been offered the option of choosing between that home and another, I would have walked out immediately.

"Well, I better get going," said the social worker, rising from the sofa.

"When will we see you again," I asked anxiously.

"I'm not sure," she replied. "They'll probably assign you a new case worker. But if not, I'll be back to check on you soon." Saying good-bye, she backed out the door, pulling it closed.

That was the first and last time we sat in the living room. In fact, we were instructed to only use the kitchen entrance. It was a five bedroom house with a formal dining room, living room and den. On every piece of furniture in the living room and dining room, was an invisible sign that said, "Don't come near me!"

"Let me show you your room and the rest of the house," said the woman, walking briskly ahead of me.

"This is my room," she stressed, pointing to a closed door while looking straight ahead. "This is my daughter's room," she said, continuing her same pace. "She's fifteen and she'll be home a little later. And this is your room, Robert. We converted a room in the attic for your brothers."

The house belonged to her parents whom she had apparently coerced into taking care of us, allowing her to continue enjoying her freedom.

"What time are we going to eat dinner?" I asked, sheepishly.

"That's up to my mother, she's the cook." Her curt response left me wondering if she was disappointed with us or was this merely her personality. Unlike her parents, who were kind and thoughtful, she was insensitive, inconsiderate and self-centered. Obviously, her heart was not in being a foster parent.

My first night's sleep was miserable. The springs supporting the mattress were so worn that the center of the bed sunk in, even when no one was lying on it. All night long I tossed and turned trying to get comfortable. I could feel a tightness in my back. In the morning I asked if I could get a better mattress, but the woman claimed it was the only mattress that would fit the bed. So, the next night I decided to join my brothers in the attic. I waited until I thought everyone was asleep, then climbed the stairs.

As I entered the room, the tiny attic window deprived my eyes of the moonlight. I nearly stumbled over my youngest brother, Maxie, who was asleep on the floor next to the bed. I remembered Freddie telling me that Maxie had fallen off the edge of the bed the night before. Freddie, like many kids, was a bad sleeper. He would toss and turn throughout the night; therefore, one full-size bed was not large enough for the three of them.

I wasn't sure whether he pushed Maxie off the bed unknowingly or deliberately because of Maxie's habitual bed wetting. I lifted Maxie from the floor, removed his wet pajama bottoms, placed him under the covers at the foot of the bed and curled up next to him sideways.

As I lay there thinking of the many changes my little brothers had been through since our mother died, I hoped that they would be able to handle all of the changes that were undoubtedly ahead of them.

It was summer time and in search of friends I would leave home after breakfast and return in time for dinner with no questions asked. With this foster mother, the motto seemed to be: *I won't bother you if you don't bother me.* What a contrast! Life in the orphanage was structured and routine. We went to sleep by a bell, got up by a bell, ate by a bell and had no freedom. But here in this foster home which afforded us no freedom while inside the house, they could care less what took place outside of it. She made no attempt to hide the fact that she was our guardian—period.

On the Road Again

One day while playing in the yard my ball went over

the neighbor's fence. When I climbed up to see where it was, the kid next door, who was around twelve years old, yelled at me to get down off of his fence. I asked him to throw the ball back over, but he refused and continued playing. I don't remember what I said to him next, but I'm sure it was threatening in nature. However, I do remember his next words, which were, "Go to hell with your stinkin' Momma."

That was probably the worst thing he could have said to me. I reached down and picked up the nearest rock and hurled it in the direction of his face. His scream was horrifying. He grabbed his left eye with both hands and ran towards his house. Before he could even reach the back porch, the screen door flew open and bursting through with an alarming look on her face was his mother followed by four older brothers. The sight of blood smeared over her son's face and his frantic behavior made her hysterical.

"What did you do?" yelled one of the boys, pointing his fist at me. I wanted to apologize and explain why it happened, but clearly they were too angry to listen to me. Knowing that most people are not able to think rationally or objectively when their loved one has suffered a traumatic experience, I jumped down off the fence and walked slowly back to my house.

"Stupid," I scolded myself, "what do you think's gonna happen to you now? You'll probably end up in a reform school. This woman you're staying with is not gonna stand up for you. She doesn't even know you and doesn't seem to want to. Plus, she and her next door neighbors have probably been friends for years."

The pressure in my head mounted as I considered my situation. It was by far the worst thing I had ever done and I had no one to run to. I longed for the support of a parent. Even if my foster mother had been home, I knew she would not have supported me. What I didn't know was whether or not the boy would lose his eyesight—the fear of that happening gripped me.

"Let's hope it's not serious," said the old man who was in the yard the whole time watering his garden. Shaking his head slowly, he said, "You should not have thrown the rock, but he should have known better than to say what he said."

I went to the front window and just stood there watching the neighbor's house. A short time later, their car pulled into their driveway. I couldn't see who got out, but within minutes the injured boy's four brothers came out of the house and paraded past our front window. One of them held up a sheet of notebook paper with the words, **"You're Dead,"** scrawled in red.

Shortly thereafter, my foster mother came home. After talking to her parents, she immediately headed over to the neighbor's. I waited in my room for her to return, but she never came upstairs. I heard nothing from her until late afternoon the next day when she called up to me from the foot of the stairs.

"Robert, someone is here to see you." Oh, no, I thought, the neighbors are going to kill me!

My heart began pounding through my chest. I didn't mind talking to the boy's parents, but I knew his brothers would not be reasonable and there would be no one to control them. Fearing for my life, I slowly made my way down the stairs and into the living room. Thank God! I thought, as I looked into the eyes of a well-dressed lady with a professional smile; whom I immediately knew had to be a social worker.

"Hi, Robert. I'm your new social worker. We've made arrangements for you to move in with your sisters and we thought it best to do it today."

"But what about my little brothers? They'll be all alone without me!"

"They'll be fine," she said softly. "Now go tell them good-bye and get whatever you intend to bring."

I can still see the fear in their eyes as I told them I was going away. They reacted as if I was their father being carted off to jail.

"Hurry up now," urged the foster mother, holding the boys back. "You're just making things worse by taking too long."

"Doesn't she know, I'm more than just their brother," I thought. "I link them to their past. The youngest has already forgotten our mother and the others will likely forget her soon. Who's going to help them. Who will look out for them?"

My departure was extremely painful for my brothers. Their fearful cries could be heard all the way to the car. As we pulled away from the curb, I wondered if the boys next door would retaliate by taking their anger out on my brothers.

"Please, God," I prayed, "move them to a home

where they'll be loved, comfortable and safe."

It was about a fifty minutes drive to White Plains. I really didn't feel much like talking.

"What are you thinking about? Are you angry? What happened between you and the boy next door?" The questions kept coming. At first I thought the woman was simply trying to take my mind off my brothers.

Years later I concluded that she was conducting a psychological evaluation to determine if I had a propensity for violence. Considering my state of mind at that time, I may have exhibited any number of tendencies. Whether or not her intent was to evaluate or console me, neither her words, the beautiful landscape along the Bronx River Parkway, nor the anticipation of seeing my sisters could take my mind off my brothers.

Leaving the parkway and passing through the business district, the narrow, residential streets and the sight of black kids walking along the roadside let me know that we were almost there. Finally, we stopped in front of a white, two-story house set on a well-manicured acre of land. It was everything I had ever dreamed of in a house.

The spacious yard was surrounded by oak trees with an apple tree, pear tree, plum tree and a yellow cherry tree lining the long driveway. It had a large garden with tomatoes, corn, squash, lettuce, beets, cabbage and eggplant. On guard was a large dog, part German shepherd and part collie, who growled viciously, though I could tell he couldn't wait to make friends.

I stood there marveling at the contrast between this home and the one bedroom, rat infested, tenement building we used to live in before my mother died. I recalled lying atop my bunk bed, looking at a poorly plastered ceiling, fantasizing about the day when I would present my mother with a house like this.

As we climbed the porch steps, the front door opened and a heavy-set woman in her sixties welcomed us in.

"Robert, this is Mrs. Holmes."

"Hello," I said. I could tell by her face and voice that she was an honest woman with a lot of love in her heart, but I questioned whether or not she knew how to show it. My sisters, Betty and Doris, were standing on the staircase with beaming eyes causing my spirit to revive. Clearly they were thrilled to see me, but there was something to say about their careful behavior. It hinted that living here may not be fun.

"Well, you're just in time for dinner," she said, closing the door after saying good-bye to the case worker. "The girls can show you where to put your things. The bathroom is at the top of the stairs and by the time you wash your hands and come back down we'll be ready to eat."

Of the three bedrooms located upstairs, the nicest one had a view of the west side and rear of the house. It was occupied by a renter—a traveling minister who was seldom there. The room next to it was occupied by a woman in her mid-twenties—a former foster child who spent her last two years of foster care in this very home. Previously, she had slept in the third bedroom, but after being released from county care, she asked if she could rent the middle room which was vacated.

The third bedroom was a narrow, L-shaped room added onto the front of the house, built atop the front porch. It stretched the entire front of the house and extended around the west corner approximately one-third its length. Betty and Doris slept at the west corner of the room and my bed was at the east corner. There was a large window in front of my bed, a large window in the center of the room, and a large window in front of the girl's bed. This made it the best sleeping room in the house during the summer months, but as I soon found out, winter was a monster.

"So, Betty, what's it like living here?"

"Well, I guess it's ok, but she's really strict."

"How about her husband?"

"Oh, he's nice. He never bothers us, but you can tell he doesn't play."

"The food is on the table, come on down," called Mrs. Holmes from the foot of the stairs. As soon as we came down she said to me, "Robert, I want you to know that you can call me Mommy, or Mrs. Holmes or Mother Holmes, it's up to you."

Like the sudden steep drop of a roller coaster, I was plunged into a sea of emotions that I never knew was there. "Call you Mommy?" I thought to myself. "Never!"

I'm sure she was just being courteous and meant no harm, but the idea that she would even think she could replace my mother, was to me a tremendous insult. Does she think I was left on a doorstep at birth or something? I had a mother that loved me and she died less than six months ago. I didn't come here looking for a mother, I just wanted a home and some help until I was old enough to take care of myself.

Truth is, being an apprehensive eleven-year-old orphan, I very much needed a caring mother to love and nurture me. Yet it was imperative that it be accomplished without dishonoring my biological mother's memory. Calling another woman Mommy, to me, bordered on blasphemy. I felt obligated, therefore, to insist that the word foster (which means to provide parental care and nurturing for one who is not related by blood or legal ties) always precede mother. And that the word mommy forever be retired.

"I'll call you Mrs. Holmes," I said.

"That will be fine," she replied, turning quickly toward the kitchen, with body language indicative of one slightly offended.

As we sat down to eat, I noticed a faint frown on Betty's face as she looked at her plate.

"What's this?" I asked, pointing to a healthy serving of something that appeared to be fried, but not meat.

"It's eggplant," Mrs. Holmes responded proudly. "It's fresh out of our garden; picked it today."

I had never heard of eggplant before. "Please let me like it," I thought to myself. One bite and I concurred with Betty. It was the nastiest vegetable I had ever tasted.

"I don't really care for it, may I put some back?"

"Me too," said the girls. What did we say that for?

Her husband leaned forward and said, "You kids are very fortunate to have garden fresh food and a woman who happens to be one of the best cooks in the city to prepare it for you."

"We do not waste food," said Mrs. Holmes. "Eat all of it, it's good for you." Her eyes monitored every bite, as if daring me to display any dissatisfaction.

"And before there is any misunderstanding," she continued, "let's get a few things straight. I agreed to have you all come live here; therefore, I propose to do all I can to provide you the best home. Now, Robert, I know you had some problems in your other foster home, but we're not going to put up with any foolishness here. Before you arrived the girls never complained about one solitary thing. Now, all of a sudden they don't like the food. If you're not going to behave yourself, I'll just call your social worker and have her come get you. Is that clear?"

"Yes."

"Yes, what?"

"Yes, Mrs. Holmes."

"I know it's been a difficult year for you, but there are certain rules that you will have to abide by if you intend to live in this house. As long as you live here you'll go with me to church Tuesday nights, Friday nights and twice on Sunday. On Saturdays you will have certain chores. The floors must be mopped, including the halls and the steps. The bathrooms must be cleaned along with your room and the front porch. Also, I expect you to help my husband keep up the yard. The lawn must be mowed and there are lots of leaves to be raked in the fall.

"In the evenings, my husband and I often enjoy watching the news on television. We normally leave the dial set on channel 2. I don't believe in children sitting up watching a lot of television, but when it's on you're welcomed to watch it with us. If there is something special you would like to see, let me know. We paid good money for that television and I won't have you turning the channels back and forth getting it all out of whack.

"And keep in mind that the carpet in the living room is very light and you can easily track in dirt. It took us a while to get the living room as nice as it is and I intend for it to stay that way. So, if you're not watching television with us, there is no reason for you to be in there.

"I realize it's going to take time for us to get used to each other. I want to love you and I want you to love me. Many a child has come through this home over the years. Some were more difficult than others, but I tried to love and treat all of them the same. Many of them still write me today. They always tell me that this was the best home they ever had.

"Now, I want you to be happy and I'll bend over backwards to see that you are. But I demand obedience. I will not have you running over me. You understand?"

"Yes, Mrs. Holmes."

"Alright, now go on and finish your food, then brush your teeth and get ready for church."

So, there I was, in my new home for less than an hour and already I'd been accused of inciting a rebellion, forced to eat that which I despised and threatened with relocation. One minute she suggests I call her mommy and the next minute she's threatening me with relocation. Am I dreaming? Am I just unlucky? Or, is there something wrong with me?

I believe if we could poll all ex-foster children and ask them what were the most frequently uttered, negative statements made to them; undoubtedly, at the top of the list would be: *If you don't straighten up, I'll send you back where you came from.*

There are many good-hearted, well-intentioned foster parents, who out of frustration have inadvertently made similar statements, unaware of the magnitude and cruelty of the message. I do believe Mrs. Holmes was one of them. On the other hand, there are those whose motives for parenting are questionable. They would never admit to needing the child. If anything, they commend themselves for doing the child a favor by opening up their home. If parents cannot bring themselves to acknowledge their need for a foster child, in some way the child will likely suffer and the parenting experience will be negative.

After returning from church I was more than ready for bed. Aided by the sound of crickets, I relaxed and reflected on the events of a very long day. "This is your second foster home, Rob," I told myself, "and you've got to make the best of it. The reality is, you are not in control of your life and will not be in control for at least seven years. You blew your chance to help your brothers and if you lose this home you'll be of no help to your sisters either. So what if it's not what you expected. You can handle it, eggplant and all."

Three

Labeling

*I*n 1992, I was invited by Zena Oglesby, of the Institute for Black Parenting to speak at a conference in Michigan to a large group of social workers and administrators. My purpose was to provide training on how to better assist foster and adopted children. I deliberately opened my speech in a slow, calm voice, describing my professional experiences and accomplishments. Gradually, my voice intensified as I related the painful details of my childhood and the ruinousness of labeling.

It was the first time they had ever been addressed by one who was raised in the foster care system. After just ten minutes into my speech, I stopped to take an impromptu poll. As anticipated, over **90%** of those in attendance admitted that they had already prejudged me. Their preconceived notions about foster kids, made what would normally be considered a passionate, animated speech appear to be the venting of concealed, unresolved emotions. This they conjectured from my self-revealing message and impassioned style which seemed a bit unusual for a minister.

Having the opportunity to relay information to an assembly of social workers, which could in turn enhance life for some disenchanted child, was both invigorating and gratifying. By the conclusion of my presentation, the impact was such that, before I could sit down they had invited me back to do two more seminars. The following year I was asked to deliver the keynote address for the State's annual Foster Care and Adoptions Supervisory Conference. Ironically, I was recommended by someone who had initially labeled me a fanatic.

Labeling can be ruinous. It is often a rush to judgment that destroys positive opportunities. It results from judging the entire person or some aspect of the person based on his or her actions, appearance or behavior. It's derived from limited information, misinformation, or one's own past and often negative experiences. This frequently occurs when we attempt to classify unfamiliar actions, behaviors and motives, and force them to fit within the scope of our understanding. Thereby, we decline to pursue information that would provide greater clarity.

Moron

When I was seven years old, I started playing the baritone horn and trombone. At age eight I joined the school orchestra, and at age nine I was one of two students who won a scholarship to an advanced music school run by the county. At age eleven my mother died and I never picked up a horn again. I'll have more to say about this in a later chapter.

Shortly after entering junior high school I was given an IQ test. Neglecting to consider its importance, I spent more time trying to determine if the girl at the next table was interested in me than I did trying to answer the questions. And there were other distractions, such as, comparing my lame clothing to the stylish clothing that the other kids wore. Consequently, my test efforts proved disastrous.

After correcting the test, the school counselor called me to her office and was disturbingly crass as she informed me of my score.

"Robert, your test results indicate you have the IQ of a moron. Your score was 75."

I wasn't really sure of the true definition of the word *moron*. I believed it to fall somewhere between idiot and fool. It was not a word that we, in our neighborhood, used to describe people. And likewise, many of the questions on the test used words and situations that were unfamiliar to me. The only time I recalled seeing the word *moron* was in a joke book. Question: Why did the moron throw the clock out the window? Answer: He wanted to see time fly. Instantly, the book's picture of a nerdy boy throwing a clock out of a window pervaded my mind. I thought to myself: "That's not me! Sure my grades are lower in most of my classes than they should be, but do they really think I'm retarded?"

Upon returning to class I went immediately to the dictionary to learn the truth about myself. Looking up the word moron, it read: *a very foolish or stupid person; retarded.*

The words hit me like a ton of bricks! I couldn't take my eyes off of them! My stomach muscles started arguing with my lunch and any confidence I may have had was suddenly nonexistent.

It's amazing how easily just one word from a person, particularly someone considered to be knowledgeable, can cause a person to question their own beliefs or abilities. For the next twelve years the label *moron* haunted me and hampered nearly everything I did. Simple instructions had to be repeated, and everything I read had to be read twice. Names, even names of people I may have known for years would escape me.

The knowledge that my IQ was lower than every other student in the school was unbelievably damaging. It forced me to accept, as fact, the idea that even those students who looked, talked and acted stupid, were actually mentally superior to me. Shortly thereafter, my English teacher asked me a question to which I responded, "I've already did that."

"You mean," she corrected, "I've already done that." Though just a simple correction and lovingly done, the humiliation sabotaged my vocabulary, creating a daunting expectation of failure. An intellectual conversation became something to be feared.

Only when speaking to a person of equal or lesser

intelligence would my speech have any fluency. Fear would strike whenever someone who had been to college or was on their way to college engaged me in any meaningful dialogue. If anything was said or a question asked which caused me to stall or look stupid, I would immediately begin perspiring profusely and my vocabulary would vanish.

Sadly, I was conforming to the image that was placed in my head. Students with good grades intimidated me and I even avoided conversation with my teachers. Words that I had learned, but were not part of my normal conversation, even many commonly used words went unselected, fearing they would be used incorrectly.

In my entire junior and senior high school experience, I never read a book with more than fifty pages in one sitting. I avoided any subject that required an intellect to pass. Cs and Ds were the only grades I had ever received except for Bs in Physical Education.

Being nice looking with a likable personality was the only thing I appeared to have going for me. However, diminishing confidence, dated clothing and consistently poor performance in the classroom made me look and feel lame. **Orphan** was bad enough, but having to wear labels like *moron* and *lame* made it difficult to sit in a classroom and concentrate. Each time I'd move to another city, I would attract some of the most attractive girls in the school. However, once they realized I only had one decent outfit, which was my entire wardrobe, my reputation was revised downward.

For this reason I now urge social workers and foster

parents to work together to ensure that their children, particularly teenagers, begin their first day at a new school with at least one week's compliment of clothing comparable to their peers. Had that happened for me I may have been spared a number of negative experiences.

Having lived with many falsely attached labels, my heart really goes out to children who have gotten off to a bad start. Many of whom are mere victims of heartless, frustrated adults, blindly forging their way to the illusive pinnacle of pleasure and success. Many are restless, unsympathetic and dollar driven, who see underprivileged or troubled children (particularly orphans) as neglected, inner-city paraphernalia.

Orphans are viewed with the same disdain as dilapidated buildings on valued land, over which freeways are built that spare the eyes of the prominent and the up-and-coming. Few will admit it, but this thinking has contributed much to the enthusiasm for new prisons, jails and orphanages.

To live in the richest country in the world and to dismiss inhumanness with popular proverbs like: *Only the strong survive* is nothing short of savage. Too often, adults, even those who have accepted positions which service the needs of children, fail to estimate the damage caused by oversight or indifference.

Empowering problem children requires more than just credentials. It takes a heartfelt concern that transcends one's personal need for advancement. I'll have more to say about empowerment in a later chapter.

Power

There are specific reasons why people take in foster children. It's not merely because of a great big heart that cannot bear to see a child without a home. Rarely does anyone take in children simply to meet the children's needs. Contrary to what most people think, it is the adult's needs that are most considered when contemplating foster parenting. However, if the child will only be in the home a few months, the needs of the foster parent may not be an issue. But if they accept a child for a considerable length of time, it will be primarily because **they** have a need to have that child in their home. This they may never admit. It's amazing how difficult it often is for human beings to acknowledge their need for another person, even when they feel they cannot live without them.

If I had said to my mother (when she was alive), "Mommy, you know you need me," even if she thought I was out of place, she would not have been insulted by it. But had I said those same words to any of my foster parents, no matter how I explained it, they would have regarded it as the ultimate insult. Why should a child be deprived the pleasure and security of knowing that he or she is needed? Regardless of how old or young we are, we all have this same basic human need. People who know they are needed have a certain degree of power. Invariably, a person who is not needed is powerless.

For example, when employees go on strike, it is a power-move designed to achieve a desired goal. As long as they are needed they have power. In 1988, President

Reagan sent a message to the Air Traffic Controllers, saying in essence; if you don't return to work you'll be replaced. They refused. Soon they were forced to live with the painful reality that the emergence of newly trained controllers had rendered them powerless.

Back when my mother was living I was a very empowered child. She empowered me by letting me know that I was special. I was not special simply because I came out of her womb; there are thousands of kids whose biological mothers have no love or concern for them whatsoever. But what made me special was the fact that she needed me. She needed my love, my smile, my questions. She needed me to do well in school and realize my potential, that I might go places and do things that she was unable to do. When she died my life changed suddenly.

Though I did not anticipate anyone in the orphanage or foster homes going out of their way to make me feel special, I certainly didn't expect to be threatened with eviction because I didn't like something that was cooked. My mother could always tell if her kids simply did not want to eat a particular food or genuinely did not like it. She would not have forced us to eat that which she knew we detested. Mrs. Holmes, on the other hand, did not hesitate to spout her misgivings. Ignoring my feelings and the anguish on my face, her message was clear: *I do not need you... you need me.* Painfully, I conceded that I was powerless.

Powerless people are frequently victimized both mentally and physically. They must keep their thoughts to themselves or suffer the consequences. Children who are unwanted (not special to anyone) are without question the most vulnerable. The threat of being evicted is difficult enough even for a working adult to deal with. One can easily imagine the impact on a child who is not in position to influence his or her outcome. Such threats should occur only as an exhibition of "tough love" when love is apparent (not as an exercise of anger, nor as a weapon to force compliance).

Displaying insensitivity and harsh rule, while subtly driving home the message, *you need me*, will likely insight indignation which may persist for years. *Webster* defines indignation as: *Intense, deep felt resentment or anger aroused by annoyance at, displeasure with or scorn over something that actually is, or is felt to be unjust, unworthy or mean.*

The indignant individual will find it nearly impossible to receive advice or instruction from the person who prompted the indignation. Therefore, if a foster child is denied the love, attention and freedom he or she feels is deserved, it will likely cause resentment and defiance which will eventually result in the child being labeled. Many foster kids, like myself, have been victims of false labeling passed on by case worker to parent without considering how the information may be processed.

Commitment

Opening one's home to a stranger is a major undertaking which may drastically alter a family's normal routine. There are high hopes that the new child will fulfill a particular need that exists in that home.

Frustration, anger, even bitterness can easily surface if after going through extensive preparations to receive a child, she does not work out. With strong feelings and emotions, it's easy, whether intentionally or unintentionally, to falsely label a child, especially if the parent's dreams were crushed.

Labels occur automatically when there's no justifiable reason for relinquishing a child; and the foster parent, in order to acquire another child, must maintain a favorable relationship with the agency. Therefore, workers should exercise caution and wisdom when sharing with a new foster parent unconfirmed, negative information contained in a child's records. The file should contain an accurate representation of the child's condition and not merely a label passed on by an unhappy parent.

It's unfortunate, but the reality is that the pressures of this age have produced impatient and intolerant people capable of only a shallow commitment, contingent upon their own personal happiness. We see this lack of commitment reflected in areas such as the divorce rate, and disturbingly in the number of foster children repeatedly displaced. Some have experienced more homes then they have birthdays. Change in itself is tough enough, but it is particularly devastating for foster children who often experience it suddenly and repeatedly.

Recently, I talked to a seventeen year old girl who, at the time, was trying to adjust to her seventeenth foster home. This is a shame. If a child clearly has a problem which renders the parent helpless, then certainly the child should be moved and the new foster parent informed of the details. But problems arise when workers share the opinions of previous foster parents, which will likely be accepted as fact simply because it came through the lips of a trained professional. The parent assumes that if it were not true, the worker would not have mentioned it.

I do not mean to discount the value of a parent's findings which could very well equal or even be more accurate than the professional's. But, just as we do not relate a dream as if it were an actual occurrence, we should not share another's unconfirmed opinion as if it were the results of a thorough evaluation by a licensed expert.

Anyone can appreciate the loving, obedient child who consistently meets their parent's needs and the needs of the family. But just as we would not forsake our biological children simply for failing to meet our expectations, we should not be so quick to renege on our obligations to foster children either. Foster parenting is not a job for selfish people; it's for those who have love, patience, interest and integrity and are prepared to make a commitment to another human being.

Truth is, you may never see the fruit of your labor. Your kids may be thirty years old before they begin to apply what they've learned from you. In First Corinthians chapter 3, verse 6, Paul says:

I have planted, Apollos watered; but God gave the increase.

He was speaking to a group of prideful, impatient,

overzealous Christians who had to be reminded that all we can do is plant and water, but the increase comes from God.

It's selfishness that insists on being immediately rewarded for one's efforts. True love strives to help a person actualize their full potential. Parents may go a lifetime without seeing the fruit of their labor, but true love will leave them with no regrets.

Misunderstanding

Some parents view the problem child as a challenge and an opportunity to help shape a young life with their knowledge and love. Others feel it's their life's duty to straighten out wayward children with tough discipline. This is what caused me and Mrs. Holmes to get off on the wrong foot.

On the spur of the moment, due to the situation that occurred at my previous foster home, Mrs. Holmes was asked to take me in. The worker told her (prior to my arrival) about what I did to the boy's eye; adding that I had a strong will, and may be somewhat unpredictable, but should do well with proper supervision.

Considering how well mannered my sisters were, Mrs. Holmes probably concluded that all I would need is a little of her special brand of love and discipline. But it didn't work out that way. Because of the false label placed on me, any effort to discover what was really inside of me was abandoned. In fact, two years later, it was the false label that caused her to request that I be removed from her home.

Here's what happened. My older sister and I were in the kitchen; she was ironing and I was putting away the dishes. We were approximately eight feet apart. I can't recall what Betty did wrong, but Mrs. Holmes decided to whip her for it. As she moved angrily toward her with a switch in her hand, Betty sat the iron in an upright position and stood with her back against the wall. Realizing that the iron was hot and sitting directly in front of my sister, I decided to move it out of the way so that she wouldn't get burned.

As I picked up the iron, Mrs. Holmes gasped and cried out, "You! You would burn me with an iron? Put it down now!" Terror donned her face.

For a moment I just stood there utterly stunned at such an atrocious accusation. Her wide, staring eyes told me she was truly afraid of me.

"Go upstairs to your room and stay there!" she shouted.

The mere thought that I would burn a sixty-something year-old woman with an iron simply for whipping my sister, was unconscionable. What had I said or done to force her to draw such a conclusion, I thought. Immediately, I recalled that tragic incident at my previous foster home. I knew then that Mrs. Holmes had been told about my throwing the rock at the little boys eye and it led her to conclude that I was violent.

A few days later a social worker came by. She was fresh out of college and had recently received my case.

"I'll leave the two of you alone to talk," said Mrs. Holmes, as she went back to her crocheting.

"Robert, why don't we take a ride and talk," said the worker.

"OK, I'll get my coat." As I started up the stairs the worker followed me.

"I'd like to see your room," she said eagerly. I knew she was in for a surprise.

Entering the room, she asked, "Why is it so cold in here? When do you turn on the heat?"

"Heat? There is no heat," I said.

"You mean you all have been sleeping in this room throughout the winter with no heat?"

"That's right," I responded. She appeared astonished.

"How are you able to stand it?"

"Well, you get used to it. We use extra blankets and wear long pajamas, sweat shirt and socks."

Shaking her head in disbelief, she turned to go back downstairs. Right about that moment, Mrs. Holmes yelled from the base of the stairs, "What are ya'll doin' up there?" She was visibly upset. As we walked down the stairs, she said, "There's no reason to inspect my house. Why didn't you let me know you wanted to go upstairs?"

"I really hadn't planned to go up there," replied the worker, "but I didnt think it would be a problem."

"Well, I just want to know before people go roaming through my house. I've been keeping kids for fifteen years and none of the other workers saw a need to go upstairs."

"I apologize," said the worker, while putting on her gloves. "We won't be gone long."

As we walked to the car I thought to myself, "Boy oh

boy, why me. Either way it goes, I lose. There is no way
Mrs. Holmes will ever believe that I did not ask the worker
to inspect the bedroom."

Nothing was said as we drove off. It seemed the social worker was collecting her thoughts, choosing her words
carefully.

"Why did you not mention the fact that you had no
heat in your room to your previous case worker?"

"I didn't know what she would say. I didn't know if
she would even try to help us."

"What do you mean? Why would you question
whether or not she would help you?"

"Well, I'm sure she would have done something, but
I'm not sure if I would have been better off because of
it." She seemed puzzled by my response. I couldn't tell if
her blank stare meant compassion, irritation or empa-
thy.

"Well, all I know is that my first case worker dropped
me off at an orphanage and told me she would return the
next day. It took weeks. The second worker told Mrs.
Holmes that I might be a problem because of what happened at my first foster home. And because of that, Mrs.
Holmes was unnecessarily hard on me. The third worker
seemed to like Mrs. Holmes and felt that I was very fortunate to be in her home.

"Not knowing how you felt, I wasn't sure what you'd
do with my complaint. I wasn't sure if you would tell
Mrs. Holmes and simply leave me there to be punished.
Would you have sent me to another city to experience
possibly the same thing? Would I have to get used to a

new home, different foods, different rules? Would I have
to go to a new school, prove myself to new classmates and
try to make new friends? When considering all the possible, negative consequences, the cold room seemed to be
a better option."

It is not uncommon for foster children to tolerate
unfavorable or even abusive conditions and not tell their
case workers. Social workers are often viewed, somewhat,
like real estate agents. The agent has a relationship with
both the buyer and the seller, but an allegiance with the
seller. If they do not please the seller, they will lose the
listing and commissions.

Likewise, the social worker has a relationship with
both the foster parents and the child. Yet, the worker's
allegiance is with the foster parents, because by them the
worker's case load (number of waiting children) is re-
duced.

Most older foster children understand this and therefore, will only tell a case worker that which they are willing to have their foster parents hear. God only knows how
many foster children endure unpleasant relationships and
suffer all manner of abuse; fearing that speaking up would
only exacerbate their situation.

Poor Match

Of all the boys who had lived with Mrs. Holmes,
only one was actually looking for someone to call mother.
She had always wanted a son. You could hear her pain
each time she repeated the story of how they took from

her the sweetest little boy, who loved her and called her Mommy. She had a tremendous need to be needed, but her strict ways made it difficult for kids to get close to her. Having ample room she would usually be asked to take in sets of siblings. Furthermore, over the years she came to depend upon the additional income.

It was clear what she wanted from me but I just did not have it to give. Our communication was further hampered by the fact that she had initially labeled me "a problem." In frustration she would often say, "You're just head strong. You think you're gonna have your way, but you're not." Her chiding only fortified my feeling of powerlessness. We both knew within the first hour of my arrival at her home that happiness was probably unattainable. The most either one of us could hope for was peace.

Trying to Survive

At age fourteen I was moved again; this time, into the same city that my brothers had just been moved to. It was my first day at a school which had the reputation of being the roughest in the county. They placed me in a class with some of the school's most infamous characters. I remember it as though it were yesterday.

The class was enjoying a lively discussion when suddenly yours truly, decked in a greenish-blue, iridescent, nehru jacket with velvet collar entered the room. Then there was silence. I watched their eyes move from my jacket down to my shoes. My slim, black pants which stopped just short of my shoes were lightly shining on the

thighs from over pressing. I placed myself two chairs behind two of the cutest girls I had ever seen. The one on
the left, Linda, one of the school's best athletes, gave me
a look indicating that we may soon have a problem.

Class dismissed without a word being said to me, but
before the week was out they were using me for laughs—
and the trend was growing. Leading the charge was Linda;
never missing an opportunity to be rude and becoming
more antagonistic each day. I couldn't figure out what
was wrong. (She obviously didn't like me, but why?)

I later learned the shocking coincidence that her boyfriend, who was quite popular, was a foster child and
lived in the same home as my brothers. When last I talked
to them they mentioned him and said he was having problems. Could it be that his foster mother told him about
me, and that she had been asked to take me in? Could
she have threatened him with "straighten up or be replaced" and he, in turn shared it with Linda?

My back was truly up against the wall. The worst
thing a guy could ever do is go to a new school and get
into a fight with a girl. On top of being the target of every
guy in the school, you'd certainly have to fight the girl's
boyfriend. That's something I didn't want to happen because whether I won or lost, I didn't know what her boyfriend would attempt do to my brothers. "Rob, you better derail this train soon," I thought, "before it gains too
much momentum."

Insults from the guy sitting next to me were getting
on my nerves. He was somewhat bigger than me, but I
could tell he was a "wanna be" and not a major player. I

decided to use him to make a statement. Within minutes he slapped me with another sarcastic remark. Without saying a word I got up, overturned his desk (desk-chair combination) with him in it, landed two solid blows to his nose, drawing just enough blood to give cause for concern, then held him down until the teacher broke it up.

The students didn't say a word or lift a finger to stop it. After a visit with the principal I was given the day off. The next day, as anticipated, the whole class had a different attitude toward me. Along with earning myself another false label, the toughest guy in the class wanted to be my friend. Before long I was hanging out at the pool hall, running with the street teachers and being conditioned to survive in a subculture.

Speak Up

At the close of the school year my social worker came to visit and informed me that my sister, Betty, was being moved to Harlem. I couldn't believe it.

"You mean to tell me that with all the homes in the state of New York, the only place you can find to put my sister is with a single woman in an apartment in Harlem?"

"Unfortunately, yes. No one wants a sixteen year-old girl."

"Why is that?"

"Because they believe that sixteen year-old girls, particularly those who have been moved around to different homes, are usually boy crazy and difficult to control."

"Well, we have an extra room here, let her come live with us."

"We can't."

"Why not?"

"Because your previous foster mother, Mrs. Holmes indicated that the two of you should not be placed together, for you have a tendency to gang up on the foster parent."

"Why would she say that?"

"When she attempted to discipline your sister you tried to burn her with an iron."

"What!? Are you serious?"

I couldn't believe that intelligent, educated people would attach such a label to children based solely on a presumption. "Is there anything you can do?" I begged.

I pleaded with my foster mother, Mrs. Arnell, to let Betty come live with us and she agreed. The next day I boarded a bus and traveled to the welfare office and demanded to see a supervisor. After talking to her and getting no satisfaction I demanded to see her supervisor. As she left the room I began praying, "Make them say yes, Lord."

A few minutes later, a pleasant looking lady with salt and pepper hair entered the room and sat across from me. I could tell by the way she carried herself she had the power to make decisions. I knew this was my last chance and convincing her would not be easy. I had to be humble enough to dispel the illusion that I had a propensity for violence, while at the same time display just enough anger to communicate the fact that I would not take no for an answer. It turned out to be one of my most valued experiences. Her words, "Ok, you've convinced me," not only provided a reprieve for my sister, but allowed me to esteem myself as one capable of successfully accomplishing a difficult mission.

Nurturing

As said earlier, labeling destroys positive opportunities. Had I not intervened, anything could have happened to my sister. It's absurd to assume that girls are wild and promiscuous simply because they've lived in a foster home. What some may consider "raging hormones" is often nothing more than a need for nurturing.

Webster defines "nurture" as: *To supply with food, nourishment, and protection; to educate; to give moral training to; discipline; to further the development of. The process of bringing up.*

The word "foster" means: *Sharing nourishment, upbringing, or parental care though not related by blood or legal ties. Brought up by someone other than one's natural parent.*

Nurturing is a need, as is clothing, shelter and rest. As soon as possible after a woman delivers her new born, the child is handed to her so that bonding through nurturing can begin. If the mother is not able or willing to take her child, nurturing will be provided by a nurse. Wrapped tightly in a blanket with one hand at the upper back and neck and the other at it's bottom, the child is laid gently against her chest.

Therefore, the front of the child is covered by the nurses body, it's back is covered by her hands as her tender voice speaks lovingly. All children, like infants, need nurturing. If children do not receive it they will spend the rest of their life searching for it, and it will be a major factor in all close relationships.

Unfortunately, for many, the closest thing to the nurturing experience is sex. It's perceived as the only way to force one's total attention onto themselves; having the front of their body flat up against another, their back covered with arms, while being caressed tenderly with loving words of affection.

Please do not misunderstand me. I am in no way endorsing or justifying fornication. Solomon said: *With all thy getting get understanding.* Truth is, many youth who appear to be wild and promiscuous are endeavoring to satisfy a basic need for nurturing. Because nurturing is in fact a need, they have no shame pursuing what they perceive as love. As their search affords them experiences they may long to forget, eventually they will learn that only true love leaves no regrets.

The Jerk

A friend told me about a job opening for a dishwasher at a swanky restaurant. It was located in a small, upscale town about twenty minutes north of New York City. With working papers that allowed me employment at age fourteen, I got the job.

Next door to the restaurant was an expensive jewelry

store. Each day, I would have to take dinner to the store owner—a very wealthy, elderly, Jewish man who would usually bombard me with questions involving some complicated or controversial issue. Every once in awhile he would ask me to run a special errand for him after work. One day, as I was delivering his dinner, he said to me, "Rob, rarely do I meet a youngster who is able to argue a point as intelligently, as convincingly and as cordially as you do. Have you ever thought about becoming an attorney?"

"No, I haven't."

"I'll make you a deal," he said. "If you complete two years of college with good grades, I'll cover your expenses for the remaining two years and then put you through Fordham Law School. I'll pay full tuition along with rooming and books. Just promise me that you'll finish and become an attorney."

At first I couldn't believe my ears, but the look on his face let me know that he was serious. For a quick moment I imagined myself standing in a court room in a pinstripe suit giving closing arguments before a jury. Then reality kicked in. With an IQ of 75, I couldn't get into any college, much less Fordham Law School. Not to mention the fact that I hadn't had any of the required college prep classes.

The jeweler was waiting for my response, but I didn't have the nerve to tell him what I was thinking. I pretended as if I didn't believe him. I simply chuckled and walked away.

For the rest of the day and even while lying in bed,

all I could think of was the jeweler's offer. I needed advice, but there was no one to turn to. In order to explain my fears I'd have to reveal my IQ, and I had enough labels already without adding *moron*. If I could only hire a tutor, I thought, I'm sure I could prepare for college.

The next day I tried to find out what a tutor would cost but no one seemed to know. My only hope was that the jeweler would perceive my dilemma and help me find a tutor. When I arrived at work, my boss, a close friend of the jeweler, seemed to gaze at me, puzzlingly. I was sure it had something to do with his friend's offer, but I didn't know if it was my response to it, or the fact that it was even made. Tension mounted as the time to go next door neared. What if he doesn't perceive my problem? What if he does and decides to call the school inquiring into my records?

Since my mother died, he was the first person to compliment me for having a brain. I could not bear the thought of him hearing the word *moron*. As I entered his store I instantly noticed that his demeanor was different. His usual gleam was replaced with disillusion. It must be because of my failure to respond, I presumed. He's probably saying to himself: How incredible! You offer a poor orphan boy the gift of a lifetime, and he doesn't say thank you or even acknowledge what was said.

My grip on logic was slipping. In the past, only a customer would have prevented him from talking to me—this time, he barely looked at me. Either he called and got information on me from the school or my boss told him something very negative about me. I was so embarrassed. I turned immediately and walked out assuming that he had lost interest in me.

Guilt is the weapon of choice for self inflicted, emotional wounds. "Jerk, idiot, fool," I scolded myself. "Whatever negative stereotypes this man may have ever had about black people, you've not only substantiated them, but have succeeded in taking ignorance to a new level."

Pain, like a leach, kept eating at me. The next day I called in sick, then decided not to go back anymore. I never saw the jeweler again. Convinced I could not get to college, I settled for being cool. I pretended to be content with my new label, conferred by my streets teachers. Just like all the others, it too was false. Clothes, girls and parties became the order of the day. Still, through my beveled glass view of the future, I could see that the fast lane was not the life for me. I may have lost some confidence in myself; even integrity, but not hope.

Shortly after entering high school I met with a career counselor who asked me what classes I would like to take. I told her I didn't know.

"Do you like math?" she asked.

"No, I hate math." I didn't really hate it, I was simply afraid of it. Math required a brain, the likes of which I didn't have.

"Do you like science?"

"No."

"Do you plan to go to college?"

"Not right away."

How I wished I was smart enough to go. By the close

of our session she had concluded that the best choice for me was Food Trades. I spent my sophomore and junior years rolling dough and dicing carrots.

False Labels

Any idiot can label a person. It requires nothing more than an opinion and does not need to be accurate in order to stick. When people are labeled, as with a bottle of medicine, for example, accuracy is crucial.

A label should not change from one day to the next— it should be reliable and conclusive. If it changes, it obviously was not accurate in the first place. A man having shaved his head clean may be referred to as having a bald head, but he's not labeled *bald* until his hair has ceased to grow. If a person breaks a leg we don't label that person disabled even though temporarily she is. In fact, with any injury or affliction, the label is attached only when there's permanence. A false label, though unintentional, is not only dangerous but questions the integrity of the labeler.

Proper evaluation is key when dealing with emotional or mental problems. Yet, labeling and classifying are different. To classify is to sort: simply to place in certain categories. This will make it easier to identify and track like traits and behaviors. Such classifications are often temporary as people get well, mature or find some other motivation for change.

But labels, on the other hand, connote permanence and are attached to a person by someone who does not expect that person to change. Change may or may not occur, but such negative expectations have made labeling the most commonly used method of discrimination. It is equally as destructive if placed on one's own self—it can lead to depression, criminal behavior or even suicide.

Of course, comprehending the ugliness of labels may be difficult particularly for those who have never been forced to wear one. People come to the table with biases which may affect their judgment. What one person labels as lazy may actually be disinterest. Extreme caution may be mislabeled as paranoia and confidence as conceit. We must be very careful when labeling people because self-esteem can be easily damaged and positive opportunities easily destroyed. If the person in question disputes or resents the label, accurate or not, it should not be used.

Recently, I spoke with a friend named Wendy who was also raised in the system and had been severely abused as a child. She now has a masters degree in social work and is director of a residential treatment program for youth in New York. Ironically, it's the same place she previously lived after experiencing a number of foster homes.

A recent, devastating, emotional blow caused her to flashback thirty years to the trauma of her childhood, leaving her terribly angry and dysfunctional. She concluded that her present dysfunction stemmed from that old wound (molestation) which supposedly never healed.

Far too many people, unfortunately, are inhibited by painful past experiences, both physical and emotional. Based on Wendy's history this would appear to be the case. At the same time, many have been forced (by well meaning experts) to recall unpleasant events unnecessarily, thereby triggering problems that did not previously exist or had long since ceased. Wendy's character and accomplishments led me to believe hers was not an old wound but a series of fresh cuts (recent emotional wounds).

Wendy spent two years in a residential treatment program for youth. After receiving her masters degree from New York University, she returned to the home as Director of Admissions. As director she was able to acquire a copy of the psychological evaluations which were done on her while living there. Because she asserted that she would complete a university education and go on to get her master's degree, they labeled her as having delusions of grandeur.

They wrote: "Though her full scale IQ is of average level, her verbal skills make her appear more intelligent than she really is. She will likely have considerable difficulty performing at a college level. She is a user (manipulator) and regards herself as an adult in an environment of children. She is emotionally insecure, severely deprived, shows no emotion, unwilling to try new experiences; doubtful she will ever be able to get over her childhood abuse. If she falls in love and is happily married, she might be able to have a happy future."

For years Wendy discounted this depiction of her as worthless rhetoric, citing serious personality conflicts between her and her therapist. However, when crushed recently by an incident involving her daughter, she flashed back and began feeling and reacting like the little girl in her past. She even dared to embrace the idea that the therapist was right.

"It is extremely important that we know the truth, Wendy," I said. "Let's start with this year and work backwards to childhood listing all the events that caused you great stress." It didn't take long for her to recognize that the fresh cuts received as an adult were more than sufficient to render her dysfunctional even if she had never been wounded as a child.

It's absolutely mind boggling to me how an adult, because of bias, jealousy, prejudice or greed can deliberately misguide a helpless child. I learned, the hard way, to scrutinize any advice or counseling given by anyone who appears not to care for me. Many present day problems are the result of painful past experiences. Nevertheless, to rush to this conclusion erroneously can have enormous, long-term, negative consequences.

To tell myself that a problem which occurred 15, 20, or 30 years ago is today preventing me from functioning normally, forces me to admit that something is yet not right with me. The belief that I am inferior, permanently damaged, and unable to change will erode my confidence, my self-esteem, generate anger, and even bitterness, which may manifest in various ways, including harm to myself and/or others.

Fear of failure due to incompetence stifles any enthusiasm to move forward. There would be a tendency to conform to the label I placed on myself, thereby, becoming a victim of my own ignorance.

Surely, many would quickly draw the conclusion that Wendy never got over her past. But, is this true? There's a big difference in an old wound that will not heal and a wound that's been re-injured. If I re-injure an old wound, it may take longer but I would expect it to heal. My self-esteem would not be affected by it.

But a wound that won't heal requires on-going professional attention and may produce a host of new problems, physically, emotionally and psychologically. To experience such problems unnecessarily is shameful. To experience them as a result of a false label is deplorable and sometimes criminal.

Unless a problem is permanent, we have no right to induce people with a label, to believe their condition will not improve. This occurs, unfortunately, everyday because labeling is easy and does not require intelligence, creativity or reason; just an opinion. On the contrary, it takes love, often skill, insight, understanding, patience and interest to help a child actualize his or her full potential. This will enable them to love themselves, and that love will leave them with no regrets.

Four

The System

F or a number of years now, I've had the privilege of traveling around the country, speaking to and often training foster parents and social workers on how to understand and effectively meet the needs of displaced children.

As a chaplain for the Los Angeles County Sheriff's Department, I've spent more than twelve years counseling inmates in jails and prisons throughout the state of California. I've counseled hundreds of murderers, rapists, robbers, batterers and the like.

As the president of Loving Your Disabled Child for more than eight years, I've counseled numerous families and individuals who have experienced the challenge of raising disabled children. To date it is the only Christian based, family support and resource center for parents with disabled children in the Los Angeles County area.

Having been the host of a talk radio program for three years, I have interviewed attorneys, judges, police officers, ex-felons, psychologists, doctors, victims of crime, social workers, directors of various shelters and rehabilitation centers as well as business owners and many other professional and non-professional people.

As senior pastor of Love and Order Christian Fellowship for more than fourteen years, I've counseled hundreds of innocent victims of abuse, violence and fraud, in addition to marriage and family counseling. My experiences have afforded me considerable insight in dealing with confused, defiant, and discouraged individuals. I can recognize, understand and sometimes even relate to their dysfunctional behavior.

The Worker

Those who work in children's services are very much aware of the need for good homes for foster and adoptive children. Parents have certain needs which can only be fulfilled by the child; therefore, it is tremendously important that parent and child be well matched. This is something which is often consciously overlooked.

Most agencies attempt to screen out only those potential parents who appear unfit or whose motives are deemed negative. Too often, overburdened foster care workers, pressured to find homes, are forced to make placements that they know are not in the best interest of the child.

Foster care workers are some of the finest people in the community. They enter the field not only desiring to make a decent living, but depend largely on the intrinsic rewards that come from bringing joy and order to children's lives. Whether the goal is long-term placement or reunification of the family, the social worker has many responsibilities and people to answer to.

First, they must answer to their immediate supervisors and then any other department heads. They must deal with foster parents, court appointed attorneys, the natural parents and sometimes the natural parent's attorney. Their responsibilities include: finding homes, making the placements, monitoring the children, making the required visits, planning family visits and making court reviews. All while carrying a load of sometimes between thirty to forty cases at a time.

Add budget constraints and increased competition, and before long, the idea of pursuing the best interest of the child by matching them to the proper parent is buried beneath the priorities of the department or agency. When this happens, children become nothing more than pawns to cover salaries and operating expenses.

Many workers are disturbed by this. Some consider leaving after just one year. Truth is, despite the fact that there are many loving, sincere, caring people who work within the foster care system, the system's primary commitment is not to the children but to the system itself. Foster parents and children are often sought with the same ambition that life insurance salespersons seek customers.

In other words, most of the commission is received

on the front end of the sale; once the sale is made, interest in the insured begins to dwindle considerably. After
about thirteen months or so, it may matter very little to
the salesperson what happens to the client (the money
has already been made). And so it often is with foster
children. They provide job security making it possible for
salaries and overhead to be paid. Yet, at the time of emancipation, when they really need support, advice and assistance, they are often ignored and in some cases even
denied the assistance needed to get off to a good start.

The Problem

When an athlete competes (informally) against an
inferior contestant, it is customary to offer the inferior
person a "spot" (handicap) in order to even his chances
of winning. Children in the system who are ready for release should receive no less consideration before being
thrust into the American "rat race." For many young
people, achieving success without a "spot" is highly un-
likely.

Unfortunately, it takes money to "spot" an emancipated (freed) minor; therefore, such considerations are
rarely entertained. Short of a disease, governments are
traditionally apathetic toward funding social programs.
An emancipated minor starter program would almost certainly meet resistance. This, to me, is so ironic given the
high number of youth who emancipate from foster care
and then end up in adult correctional facilities.

Surprisingly, while writing this book, I could not find

hard data from any source, be it federal, state, or local governments, universities, or any agency, providing numbers on those who leave the foster care system and enter the adult correctional system. Neither could I find anyone who had knowledge of current research in this area.

So, the questions remain. What impact does displacement have on children? Is the effect of neglect, abuse, or belittlement by one's own relatives any different when coming from those with whom she is not related? There are so many variables to consider in answering these questions. Nevertheless, these and other questions must be answered if we are to provide the best care for our youth while they are in the system and prepare them for success once they leave it.

Some progress has been made in preparing youth for emancipation, for example, the Independent Living Program. However, this involves a relatively small percentage of youth, and in many cities it's still unavailable. Attention must be brought to this issue. As long as it's viewed as insignificant, it will continue to receive low priority.

For years I've spoken to audiences around the country emphasizing the magnitude of this problem, which I've learned more about after talking to literally thousands of inmates in jails and prisons throughout California and other states since 1983.

Inmates would often come to me after hearing of my past and tell me of their foster care or group home experiences. A number of years went by before it dawned on me that there may be a correlation between child displacement and incarceration. To determine if a correlation existed, I surveyed individuals outside of the prison who after living in foster homes, group homes or other institutions, ended up behind bars.

I discovered that out of the eighty African-American males questioned who had been displaced by the system, **sixty percent** had at some point been incarcerated. Arguably, there may be any number of reasons or issues surrounding their incarceration and may have nothing at all to do with displacement.

However, if these numbers do prove to have validity, would not such knowledge demand that steps be taken to avert the inevitable? The prevailing wisdom seems to be: increase the prison budget and put more cops on the street. We have the ability and the resources to do a lot more than just that. We need leaders who are not only intelligent but have courage, compassion, good character and a strong commitment to improve life for all the people they serve.

The attention being placed on the problems with the welfare system as a whole, is only because of the impact that welfare is having on our nation financially. We should not allow complacent leaders to neglect their responsibilities merely for the sake of convenience, to the detriment of others.

I was seventeen years old when I graduated from high school; two weeks later the social worker came by, handed me a check for $50 and told me I was on my own. Checking the classified ads in the local newspaper I found a room for rent with kitchen privileges in the home of a woman whose sons were two of the most scandalous

dope dealers in the city. They knew me from the pool
hall. They slept in the room next to mine and would bang
on the wall whenever they got high, pressuring me to in-
dulge in free heroin.

One day I met a woman who had gone to school with
my mother. After explaining my situation to her she introduced me to her husband who allowed me to rent their
basement. It was dark, dirty and had no tub or shower
but provided security and privacy. I rented it assuming
that I could go upstairs and bathe. It took me a week to
clean and paint the entire basement, for which he did
give me a reduction on the first month's rent, but I still
could not use his bathroom.

For six months I went without a bath or shower. I
would sponge bathe standing in front of the sink. I wanted
to leave but stayed only because I felt somewhat safe,
comforted by the fact that they had known my mother
whose memory I believed would cause them to look out
for me. Additionally, I knew that if I were to move I
could not afford to live anywhere other than with the neighborhood riffraff.

Having no adult to confer with, I decided to look up
my older sister's father. Surprisingly, Frank still lived in
the same East Bronx apartment that he had when we
first entered foster care. I dialed his number wondering
how he would receive me after so many years. I imagined
he'd be courteous for the first two or three minutes then
find a way to politely get me off the phone. When the
ringing stopped, a startlingly familiar voice said, "Hello."
I hadn't heard that voice since I was eleven, yet it sounded

as though it were yesterday.

"Hi, Frank?"

"Yes?"

"Uhh, my name is Robby. I'm your daughter Betty's brother, our mother was Tommie Colwell."

"Hi, Robby. How ya doin?"

"Fine." His warm response took me by surprise.

"How's Betty?"

"She's fine too. She and her best girlfriend took a trip to California and decided to stay."

"You mean she lives there now?"

"Yes. Listen, I'm calling to see if you can possibly help me. I'm on my own now and I was wondering if you knew of a place to rent that's decent and inexpensive."

"Well, where are you staying now?"

"I'm living in the basement of a guy's house. I believe he used to go to school with you, his name is Mack."

"That wouldn't be Mack Jones would it?"

"Yes."

"I've seen his basement before and at that time it was a mess."

"Yeah, but I cleaned it up, painted it, put new carpet down and wall papered the kitchen area."

"Well, why do you want to leave?"

"Well, the rent has gone up and there's no bath or shower."

"Do you have to ask Mack ahead of time to use his shower?"

"No. I'm not allowed to go upstairs."

"What? Then what have you been doing?"

"I sponge bathe in front of the sink."

"What?! How much is Mack charging you?"

"$400 a month."

"What?!" His anger was quite surprising. It provided me with an experience I hadn't had since my mother died (seeing someone get upset over the wrong that someone else was doing to me).

His next statement literally changed my life. "I thought Mack was more man than that—a real man would not have done that."

It was the first time any man had ever put into perspective for me, the moral obligations of a man as he interacts with other men, women and children. Having attended church regularly from age eleven to sixteen, I heard a lot about morals and one's obligation to his fellowman, but always in a Biblical context. I concluded, therefore, that only Christians are required to adhere to such standards, and outside of Christianity there is no such expectation.

As far as I could tell, the image of a non-Christian man, at least in my neighborhood, was one who was strong, had plenty of money in his pocket, drove a nice car, had a nice house or apartment, took no mess off of anybody, and successfully balanced his time between his wife and whoever else he was interested in.

Frank was the first non-Christian man to contradict that misconception. He was a strong man who previously served time in prison for using his fists as a weapon badly hurting another man. Yet, he was very mild mannered, easy-going, hard working and by all appearances seemed to be doing quite well. Though none of Frank's blood flowed through my veins his involvement with my mother made him family.

"On my next day off from work I'm going to take you to find an apartment," he said. The following Saturday was devoted entirely to me. By the end of the day I had a beautiful, affordable apartment which was closer to my job, and had a wealth of advice and information which still benefits me today. From that day I purposed in my heart that, whenever possible, I would be to someone else what Frank was to me—a male role model.

A real man is a caring man, and does his best to share his best with those he cares for. What happened to me after leaving foster care was not unique. Everyday, young people are turned loose with no direction, no money and no place to live, only to become easy prey for cons and perverts.

The pervert says "So what!"; the con says "Too bad!"; and the welfare system closes the file on another case, while the criminal justice system prepares itself by building more prisons. With the average annual cost of housing an inmate being $30,000, concern for fellow man and common sense dictates that every emancipated minor receive ample support from all that is available within the community.

God knew when He delivered the Hebrew people from the bondage of Egypt that it would be very easy for men to forget their deprivation and ignore the God who set them free. Therefore, He gave Moses ten commandments to be given to the people along with a large list of do's and don'ts so they would honor God and respect one another. Knowing how easily men may neglect the needs of children, especially those who do not belong to them, the following declaration was included:

Ye shall not afflict any widow, or fatherless child. If thou afflict them in any wise and they cry unto me, I will surely hear their cry; and my wrath shall wax hot, and I will kill you with the sword.

Exodus 22: 22-24

A number of laws were also established; among them the law of gleaning. Glean means: *to gather up, to pick up, such as with grain, grapes or other produce or plants.* Those who did the gathering were called reapers. While harvesting they were instructed not to scrape the vines clean, but leave a little behind for the poor, the fatherless, the widow, the stranger.

When thou cuttest down thine harvest in thy field, and hast forgot a sheaf in the field, thou shalt not go again to fetch it: it shall be for the stranger, for the fatherless, and for the widow: that the Lord thy God may bless thee in all the work of thine hands. When thou beatest thine olive tree, thou shalt not go over the boughs again: it shall be for the stranger, for the fatherless, and for the widow. When thou gatherest the grapes of thy vineyard, thou shalt not glean it afterward: it shall be for the stranger, for the fatherless and for the widow. And thou shall remember that thou wast a bondman in the land of widow. And thou shall remember that thou wast a bondman in the land

of Egypt: therefore I command thee to do this thing.
Deuteronomy 24: 19-22

It's easy to understand how those born with a silver spoon in their mouths may find difficulty empathizing with the unfortunate. But many of our present leaders come from families who were once in bondage to poverty, discrimination, manipulation, etc. These we must admonish as God did Israel: Remember you too were once in need of deliverance.

Remember this Mister or Madame President when preparing the nation's budget. Remember this Governors and local officials while harvesting the field of available federal, state and county funds. Instruct your reapers not to scrape the vine, but leave something behind for the fatherless.

I believe that one of the reasons this nation has suffered such spiritual and moral decline is because God will not bless any nation that exploits, oppresses or neglects its children, particularly those who are fatherless.

When an individual is released from the military, the government anticipates the difficulty of trying to acclimate to civilian life. Therefore, benefits are provided such as The Montgomery GI Bill, The Army College Fund, small business loans, hospitalization, priority consideration for civil service jobs, special rates on home loans, etc.

Present foster care policy in most states provides nothing to help an eighteen year-old get started in life. One may argue that the military is available to everyone. This is true, but although it's available, there are many people who for many reasons do not qualify for military duty. Regardless of whether they do or don't, the military should not be one's only alternative.

At a conference a woman said to me, "There are many programs and benefits that they can take advantage of; it's on them, they have to want it." Another worker said, "I let all my kids know what's available to them."

I thought to myself, this sounds good, but if they could see through my eyes they would understand the affect that years of powerlessness can have on the mind. Whether prior to or while in foster care, painful memories, abuse, neglect or rejection, coupled with repeated and sudden changes of environment can leave children "dog paddling" in a sea of pessimism. Though able to keep their heads above water they may have never learned how to swim.

Foster children should be taught (by someone capable of getting their attention) about the importance of participating in available programs and taking advantage of certain benefits. We cannot expect an eighteen year-old, particularly one from a confused or troubled background to have a mature perspective on life. Many adults have no idea what to do with their lives until well into their thirties or older. To expect an eighteen year-old to have the insight and fortitude necessary to procure all available benefits is unrealistic.

If we really care about the future of foster children, we'll admit our failures, begin to think creatively, and draw from the vast pool of untapped resources readily available to us. For example, there are many adults who were raised in the system, who would be more than willing to volunteer their services to help in any way they can. There are church members, college students, even businesses that would get involved.

There is so much more we can and should do. In addition to housing and job assistance, I believe every young person should have an exit interview, a physical examination, and be given information and instructions as to how they should proceed.

So What!

As members of this "results oriented" society, we need to realize that there is more than just, what we call, "the bottom-line." Often that bottom-line is not the bottom at all, but merely a line drawn in haste with tunnel vision, overlooking (sometimes deliberately) important details affecting others.

For many leaders and people in general, the bottom-line is money. Fortunately, there are still some leaders whose "bottom-line" is meeting the needs of the people they serve. If ever they recognize a legitimate need among their clients, all due diligence is given to resolve it. On the contrary, those whose primary focus is making or saving money may respond by saying, "We'll see what can be done about it"; while in their hearts they are saying, "So what!"

Saying "so what," though sometimes justifiable, usually reflects a negative attitude resulting from complacency, ignorance, rebellion, or immaturity. To respond with "so what!" is to say, in essence: I'm not moved by what has or has not been done, nor by any threats or complaints; and I don't believe that anyone will make me regret my actions or position.

The fruit of this attitude has been divorce, unemployment, incarceration, hospitalization, even death. It has caused remarkable problems for many innocent people—particularly those who depend on social services.

You may be familiar with the biblical account beginning in Exodus chapter 5, wherein God sent Moses to tell Pharaoh to let the Hebrew people go. Verse one reads: *Thus saith the Lord God of Israel, let my people go.* Pharaoh responded with: *I know not the Lord, neither will I let Israel go.* By his response he was in essence saying, "So what! Who cares!" As far as he was concerned, God was non-existent and the Hebrew people served no other purpose but to carry out his own personal wishes.

It's amazing how many people think of others in this same way. This is often the way children view their parents, husbands and wives view each other, employers view employees and prison guards view inmates. Pharaoh, just like many of us, needed to be reminded that **everyone is important to someone and we all are important to God.** It makes no difference what our status is, what we look like, or how we behave—there is somebody who wants to see us live happily and prosper.

Each time Moses would approach Pharaoh with the message from God, Pharaoh refused to cooperate and

was finally forced to humble himself by a series of dreadful plagues. It wasn't until after the tenth plague (the
Death Angel) destroyed all the first born of Egypt (those
who had no blood covering) that Pharaoh agreed to do as
God had said.

Too many of us have learned the hard way that God
is able to change our attitude. Many people are incarcerated, lonely, hospitalized, divorced or unemployed because they said, "So what!" at a time when they should
have been demonstrating humility, exercising wisdom and
patience, and heeding sound advise. It makes no difference how much money we have, how many people we
have control over, the attractiveness of our bodies or how
well we speak; at some point we all will discover that the
bottom-line is actually drawn by God and it's a "line"
that does not fluctuate.

A positive attitude is a caring attitude. The attitude
of most people is: The bottom line is where I say it is,
therefore, it doesn't matter what anyone else thinks. This
is the answer of a poor conscience and flawed character.
Good character is essential for proper understanding of
the issues of life and the needs of others, and is far more
useful than a high IQ in bringing about a resolve.

Powerlessness

Ironically, in most of our nation's schools, the goal is
to impart knowledge and to teach students how to reason.
No effort is expended to develop character, or to motivate
those who are powerless. Without motivation one is bound
to fail.

Motivation comes from within, derived from an expectation of success based on previous success. Powerlessness stems from an expectation of failure. It will inevitably have an adverse effect on one's actions and decisions and may, as with me, continue to do so for many years to come.

With repeated successes comes surging confidence; with repeated failures comes disinterest. Unfortunately, our present educational system is designed to advance only motivated students. Consequently, too many students (many of whom live in the inner city) are knowingly disregarded.

There are, of course, reasons why things happen and these reasons should be explored thoroughly by people who care, to ensure equal opportunity for all.

Drug use, poverty, stress, moral decline, the breakup of the family, etc., have produced a plethora of powerless young people receiving less than the standard of care in the community. We must not forget that powerlessness, for the most part, is a present state and speaks nothing of one's potential. All it takes is a little creativity, a little guts and a lot of interest to help motivate and educate even those who are chillingly disinterested.

Just as the welfare and educational systems have serious flaws, the criminal justice system is badly crippled. The crutch on which it limps is called plea bargain. It has turned out to be an unscrupulous tool of manipulation, ranking close to the top of the system's list of barbarities.

If a person provides clear proof that he will not change

even if his current situation does, and continues to ignore the law, then by all means lock him away. On the other hand, if his behavior reflects an ignorance which is typical of one who has been relegated to poverty and dependency, unable to shake his past and ill-equipped to shape his future, then we should diligently pursue effective alternative solutions which ultimately would serve the best interest of everybody.

It's better to help shape one's future than to shackle a person to their past with a label. There are many young men and women rotting in jails and prisons today, whose downward spiral did not begin with disrespect for the law, but with a desperate attempt to overcome powerlessness.

One of the most powerless people I've ever known was a friend of mine named Lee. Like me, he was sixteen and also lived in foster care. His biological mother walked off and left him when he was nine. The foster home he lived in was run pretty much like a prison. He was treated so harshly it offended even me.

I'll never forget that warm Saturday night when Lee, myself and two other friends decided to go to a party in the South Bronx. While there, we learned about a better party across town which was a forty-five minute subway ride and then a ten minute walk. As we headed back to the subway, one of the guys, Ray, noticed keys in the ignition of a late model Chevy Impala with the doors unlocked.

"Hey man, leave it alone," I said.

Ray was the daring, fearless type who, like his father, was not known for having a conscience. As soon as he opened the driver's door, Lee jumped into the passenger's side and scooted beside him.

"Can I drive?" Lee begged. His eyes were lit up like a six year old in front of a Christmas tree.

"No way," chuckled Ray. "Are you crazy? You know you can't drive."

"C'mon, guys, forget the car, it's not worth it," I said. "We don't have that far to go anyway."

"Man, what's wrong with you?" snapped Lee. "By tomorrow they'll have the car back. If you want to take the train, that's up to you."

Distinct was the odor of trouble. Though Lee and I were the same age, I felt like his older brother. He, unfortunately, had never been empowered by his mother and I don't believe he ever knew his father.

All boys long to drive a car, but to Lee, who had never had his hands on a stirring wheel, it was a chance to prove his manhood. Reluctantly, I got in the front seat beside Lee. On the back seat was a Bible and two children's Sunday School lessons, which reinforced my feeling that something bad was about to happen. I knew, should I be arrested, there would be no one to stick up for me.

We parked approximately two blocks away from the party. Everyone jumped out of the car except Lee.

"C'mon, Lee," I pleaded. He scooted under the stirring wheel and wouldn't budge.

"Forget him," snapped Ray. "Let the fool stay there!" I closed the door and walked away hoping Lee would follow me. Then suddenly, he pushed the gas pedal to the floor, turned the ignition and blasted the motor! I just couldn't let him kill himself and possibly someone else, so I turned around and ran back to the car. Having learned how to drive, I knew how difficult driving would be for a person who had never tried to drive, especially at night.

"What do you think you're doing?" I shouted.

"I just want to take it around the block one time, then I'll park it, I swear." I knew I was walking into the lion's den, but I just couldn't let him go alone. Not only was I concerned about the probability of an accident, but I feared if he were caught he would tell on all of us.

"Ok, I'm gonna ride with you around the block one time." My plan was to snatch the keys out of the ignition at the first opportunity. Only if he thought I was helping him would he let me get close enough to do it.

"Ok, Lee. Pull the handle down to Drive. Now slowly press the accelerator." The car lunged forward, then screeched to a stop as he slammed the brakes.

"Man! Just barely press the gas pedal!"

"Alright! Alright!"

Slowly we proceeded to the end of the block, made a slow left turn and continued to the next corner. He was all over the road. As he made the next left, he picked up more speed and got angry when I tried to help him straighten out. Two more turns to go, I thought, then I'll grab the keys. Realizing his fling was almost over, he decided to make the most of it.

Approaching the next corner he punched it. The surge was more than he expected. Losing control, he panicked and instead of moving his foot to the brake, it became frozen to the gas pedal. The car raced at about 30 miles an hour, onto the curb and crashed into a tree. When I woke up, the hood was sitting in the windshield. I could hear Lee saying, "Robby, Robby! Get Out! Get Out!"

I pushed open the door and began running toward the party. As we walked through the door, I noticed everyone grimaced when they looked at me. Then someone said,

"What happened to you?!"

"What do you mean?" I asked.

"Go look in the mirror." When I looked in the mirror, I couldn't believe it. My chin was split wide open. I could see the bone. My clothes were covered with blood, yet I didn't feel a thing. Someone offered to take me to the hospital.

Had that incident occurred today, we would be standing before a judge just as powerless in his courtroom as Lee was in his foster home. Mandatory sentencing laws passed down by unsympathetic legislators anesthetized by a desire for power and the fear of their constituents, have stripped judges of their judicial discretion—ordering them (as Lee's foster mother would order him) not to think, but to do what they are told.

They would be forced to ignore the fact that, Ray, me and Lee, though we all were wrong, have significant differences in character and attitude which should be taken into account when deciding our fate. Say what you will about Ray and Lee, but in my case, where is the wisdom in prolonged incarceration? It would only expose me to a corruptive element and make it difficult upon release to market myself in an increasingly competitive society.

It's unthinkable to believe that our leaders are not fully aware of the ramifications of mandatory sentencing, the 3 Strikes Law, and others. We will never resolve crime on the streets until we address crimes that are supported by law. Whether motivated by ignorance, anger, pressure, or something more sinister, mandatory sentencing is a crime in itself. Some people have said that one of the goals of mandatory sentencing is to eliminate the need to find jobs for, or train certain uneducated workers. They also believe it's purpose is to reduce the minority population by removing the baby makers. Absurd? Maybe so. But it's also absurd to think that present policy can continue indefinitely without major consequences.

We are all glad when menacing law breakers are locked up. Yet, there are tens of thousands of young men and women needlessly wasting their lives in prisons throughout this country, placed there by selfish, unconcerned people who scoff at the idea of rehabilitation.

Everyone who is arrested is not an animal. Many of those who wear the label, *animal*, *misfit*, and the like, are the fruit of bad decisions made by power seeking "wanna-bes" while vigorously hastening to the top. Their only goal for anyone who has been arrested (unless, of course, they are related) is to punish and render them powerless.

Shame

Recently, I did a funeral for a young gang member

assassinated by his so-called friends. The chapel was packed with approximately 250 people, mostly gang members, many of them making no attempt to conceal their weapons. I had received word that the killers were in attendance.

I knew that God would have to touch their hearts in order for me to get away with saying what needed to be said. No telling if I would ever have such an opportunity again.

Most likely many of the young men and women in the room never had the privilege of sitting at the feet of a role model receiving character building advice. Many of the youngsters probably had no one at home or among their peers to provide good direction, and probably ignored their teachers when and if they decided to go to school. Obviously, in order to learn one must hear what is being said. This funeral, therefore, was the perfect setting. I had everyone's attention and respect.

Bowing my head I prayed fervently. Then with God-given boldness I declared, "It's a shame this young man had to die, and someone must bear the shame of his death." At least thirty gang members responded instantly, screaming (silently) through body language.

I knew I was skating on thin ice and every word had to be selected carefully.

"Shame," I continued, "results from fear of humiliation and disgrace due to public exposure of one's flaws or failures. *Webster* defines disgrace: *To spoil the appearance of. To cause to seem inferior by comparison.*

"People will do almost anything to avoid disgrace.

Only God knows how many people have lost their jobs or were demoted; lost their families or sit in prison because of their own or another individual's desperate attempt to save face. Regardless of who gets hurt, they will destroy anyone or anything that threatens their reputation or prevents them from looking good. Yet, fear of disgrace can provide a powerful motivation to conform to that which is good, or evil. Choosing evil reflects weakness, choosing good requires integrity and courage.

"I pray, therefore, that all those responsible for this young man's death will be motivated by the shame of his death, to turn from their evil ways and embrace that which is good. And there is none good but God."

Never have I braved so many unfriendly eyes glaring at me at the same time. I could feel their thoughts pounding against my jaw. I thought about the suffering and shame endured by the apostles and by Jesus in effort to achieve a greater good.

...and when they had called the apostles, and beaten them, they commanded that they should not speak in the name of Jesus, and let them go. And they departed from the presence of the council, rejoicing that they were counted worthy to suffer shame for His name.

Acts 6: 40-41

Wherefore seeing we also are compassed about with so great a cloud of witnesses, let us lay aside every weight, and the sin which doth so easily beset us, and let us run with patience the race that is set

before us, looking unto Jesus the author and the fin-
isher of our faith, who for the joy that was set before
Him endured the cross, despising the shame, and is set
down at the right hand of the throne of God.

Hebrews 12: 1-2

At the conclusion of my message I felt led to give an
invitation for salvation knowing full well that people traditionally do not respond at funerals.

"There are people here who long to change," I said.
"They long to give their life to Christ but do not have the
courage to stand up in front of their friends. They need
an example. God is looking for someone with the courage
to provide that example." One by one, fourteen people
stood up to accept Christ as Lord of their life.

The Best

As a chaplain at the largest jail in the nation (the Los
Angeles County jail), I've seen thousands of men stand
up publicly and commit their lives to the Lord Jesus Christ.
"Yeah, but isn't that just jail house religion which ends as
soon as they get out?" For many, yes. But make no mistake, serving God in jail or prison is not easy. Though
there are more temptations outside of prison, more responsibilities, distractions, more reasons to sin, there is
far more confusion and opposition within it.

Yet, in spite of the evidence, and knowing full well
the power that a belief in God can have in rehabilitating
an individual, there is a large element in our society who

are relentless in their efforts to nullify the influence of the church. Many of them possess some of the brightest minds in the country. Yet, for resolve, they foolishly look to a government that has no track record of success.

There's no quick fix. However, there are things we can do to pave the way for change. We can open our hearts and minds making room for people other than just those who are talented, outstanding, or gifted. The idea of a society consisting totally of people with high IQs led Hitler to slaughter millions of intelligent, innocent Jews. We must revisit history and the lessons learned from Hitler's obsession with superiority. When you can appreciate only what you consider to be the best you end up despising the rest.

A high IQ can be a tremendous asset in searching out a cure for a deadly virus. But it won't prompt a person to tell the truth, love their spouse, treat family, friends, co-workers with respect; honor their word, respect the law or deal fairly with those less fortunate. This requires character, not talent or special aptitude.

According to *Webster*, the word, gifted, means: *One who is endowed by nature or by training with a gift. It's having special talent or desirable qualities; superior intelligence; outstanding; notable.*

In essence, it's to be one of the best. We Americans are taught to place high value on the best. Requiring only the best is perceived by many as a mark of class; having an appreciation for the finer things of life. Such individuals are admired, respected and sometimes idolized. The "common folk" love just to be in their presence; they feel honored because they believe "high class" people only tolerate the best. Being among them seems to somehow validate their existence, elevating them from common to class. Like slipping their foot into a glass shoe and having it fit, they can pretend, at least for the moment, that they actually are the person that onlookers see.

The word "appreciate" means: *To place high value on something.* Appreciating only the best may be necessary in competition, particularly in business or sports, but in general, scripture does not embrace this thinking and neither should we. Conversely, in scripture it's just the opposite. God is looking for people who can place the same value on a poor person as they do the rich; on a black or brown person as they do the whites; on a disabled person as one who has full health. The book of Luke chapter 4 verse 18 reads:

The spirit of the Lord is upon me, because He hath anointed me to preach the gospel to the poor; He hath sent me to heal the broken hearted, to preach deliverance to the captives, and recovering of sight to the blind, to set at liberty, them that are bruised.

It doesn't take talent to appreciate the best. It doesn't take a formal education, imagination, integrity, class, patience, peace, skill, or wisdom. Anyone who has ever had or wanted to have a dog, probably longed to have a Lassie, a Benji or a Rin Tin Tin. A dog that learns fast, responds to verbal commands and follows instructions precisely. "Go get my shoes; go get the paper; tell Tommy it's time to come and eat."

But what about the dog who won't roll over, won't sit down when you tell him; jumps all over you, barks too much, eats too much—you hate to go near him when wearing anything nice. But on that terrible night when the prowler showed up, it was that same seemingly good-for-nothing dog who suddenly became highly valued.

Likewise, any parent would love to have a gifted child; one who is easy to appreciate, work with and understand. But don't be so quick to write off the problem child. There's a lot to be learned from him and a lot of personal growth to be achieved by dealing with him. Often times, dreadful, agonizing experiences produce the most significant, positive changes; also much needed legislation.

In First Corinthians chapter 12 beginning at verse 18, Paul says:

But now hath God set the members every one of them in the body, as it hath pleased Him.

Verse 21 continues:

And the eye cannot say unto the hand, I have no need of thee: nor again the head to the feet, I have no need of you. Nay, much more those members of the body, which seem to be more feeble, are necessary. And those members of the body, which we think to be less honorable, upon these we bestow more abundant honor; and our uncomely parts have more abundant comeliness. For our comely parts have no need; but God hath tempered the body together, having given more abundant honor to that part which lacked. That there should be no schism in the body; but that the members should have the same care one for another.

We must learn to appreciate more than just the best. How many people and how many families have been destroyed because somebody made too much to do over individuals who happen to be, or appeared to be outstanding? If we're really serious about rectifying our nation's problems, particularly the violence and unrest in many of our cities, we must discourage polarization by teaching people to appreciate even people of low degree. Romans chapter 12 verse 16 says:

Be of the same mind one toward another. Mind not high things, but condescend to men of low estate. Be not wise in your own conceits.

Talking about someone to look up to, someone to admire; now that's the person, the person capable of "coming down" and recognizing that the people they are "coming down" to, have value.

Now, what about you? Are you able to place high value on the slow learner, the introvert, the hyperactive, over-talkative, super sensitive nail biter. It annoys me to think that there are people who right now sit in high places, placed there by the voters because they promised to make life better for all citizens; and yet, they despise the poor and underprivileged giving heed to them only when forced to. They focus on building a future for our nation's best— and institutions for all the rest.

Five

I Need You

C hoosing the right foster parent is extremely impor- tant for the proper development and well-being of a child. There are thousands of children throughout this country waiting for loving foster and adoptive parents. To a child, waiting for a good home feels much like waiting for an organ donor. A poor match of parent and child will result in a serious conflict of interest in which the parent will inevitably punish the child, or vice versa. Of course, it's not always done intentionally but it's always the result of unfulfilled needs.

Ideally, children are the fulfillment of the parent's basic human desire to reproduce themselves. It would, therefore, be a mistake to place children who long to be returned to their mother or father with a foster parent who needs a child to be a reflection of him or herself.

Naturally, there are times when this cannot be helped. On a short-term basis it may not be a problem but for long-term placements, proper matching must be the objective when pursuing the best interest of the child. Nevertheless, a poorly matched family can do well as long as the parent is loving and patient and both child and parent are aware of and can acknowledge their needs and differences.

There are six basic reasons why people accept foster children. Unfortunately, not all of these are positive.

1. Need to be a parent
Couples and individuals who, for whatever reason, have never had children, desire the parenting experience.

2. Need a brother or sister for my child
Couples or individuals who have children of their own, but have decided not to have anymore, desire companionship for their child.

3. Need to replenish the empty nest, or fill void.
The children are all grown, have moved out or are deceased and now the parent(s) need someone to break the monotony and liven-up the house. They need someone to help ease marital tension.

4. Need purpose and fulfillment
Parents have achieved certain objectives, acquired

material things and need someone to share it with. These are couples, or individuals who need the satisfaction and fulfillment that comes from knowing they have helped someone else or made someone happy. They have a desire to give back.

5. Need money
Parents are primarily concerned with their own security and betterment. (With this parent it's likely that, in some way, the child will suffer.)

6. Need Power
Pre-occupied with self image and personal pleasure, this person probably grew up longing for special attention. (With this parent it's likely that the child will, in some way, be damaged.)

Sharing

Foster children need more than just a roof over their heads. They also need love, security, hope and power. Anyone considering adopting or taking in foster children should not do so simply because the child needs a home, but rather because they, the parent, **need** that child in their home.

Likewise, no one should take in foster children unless they are capable of and prepared to share their love, their life, home, family, food, time, dreams, money, possessions and flaws. I could always tell within an hour of my arrival at a new foster home, whether or not that family intended to share with me. Sharing is not a reward given to someone for making us happy, but the appropriate response of a caring heart, motivated by the reasonable expectations of another.

It's imperative that we share with those we love. People look forward to having someone to share their hopes, dreams, fears, time, love, assets, body, liabilities. After years of waiting for the ideal mate, it would be difficult to speak peaceably to a spouse who refuses to share with you. If they're not sharing, for example, their hopes, fears and dreams with you, chances are they are sharing them, or will eventually share them with someone else. The same thing applies to children. Children expect to be able to share with an adult and long to do so.

For the most part, in every home there is a desire for healthy, happy relationships among all the family members. Though happiness may not endure, to consider a relationship positive there must at least be peace. To be at peace is to be whole and complete, not fragmented or wanting. Few things threaten peace within a relationship as do inequality and the refusal to share.

Sharing is the path to peace. The absence of such peace is usually evidenced by the manner in which one speaks. If a person fails to share that which is expected to be shared, those expectations will likely turn to anger making it difficult for the other person to speak peaceably.

Anger is the inner turmoil or frustration we feel when we cannot control people or circumstances. An example of this is found in Genesis chapter **37** verses **3** and **4**:

Now Israel loved Joseph more than all his children, because he was the son of his old age: and he made him a coat of many colors.

And when his brethren saw that their father loved him more than all his brethren, they hated him, and could not speak peaceably unto him.

The coat and the love that Joseph received from his father caused his brothers to have tremendous animosity towards him. This was prompted by their father's failure to share his love equally; love which they seemingly could not elicit and had every right to expect.

Sharing makes for a level playing field. In the book of Acts chapter **4** verses **32** through **35**, God instructs the apostle Peter as to how to set up the church. Knowing the potential for discord over material possessions, God required that the church have all things common:

And the multitude of them that believed were of one heart and of one soul: neither said any of them that ought of the things which he possessed was his own; but they had all things common and with great power gave the apostles witness of the resurrection of the Lord Jesus: and great grace was upon them all. Neither was there any among them that lacked; for as many as were possessors of lands or houses sold them, and brought the prices of the things that were sold, and laid them down at the apostles' feet; and distribution was made unto every man according as he had need.

By making all things equal, there are no false expectations; everyone feels included and no one feels slighted. I've heard many foster parents complain, "I don't like the way that she talks to me. I just can't seem to make that child happy." It's easy for them to recognize anger in the child but to suppose that the foster parent had anything to do with it would be unthinkable.

So often parents will require that their children open up to them, though they themselves are never candid with their children. Just as parents have needs and expectations, so do children. They have much to share and they need to share it, but will discontinue sharing if the parent will not reciprocate.

Each time a child is moved from one non-sharing home to another, he is likely to become increasingly distant and secretive. It's important, therefore, to remember that sharing is the path to peace. Of course, for true and lasting, inner peace, that path would have to lead to God.

All children need to hear parents say, "I love you." But for displaced children it's equally as important to know that **they are needed** (to know that they are not just receiving a favor). Parents must be able to say, **"I need you,"** and share that fact. Children need to hear facts such as:

- I need you because you afford me the parenting experience I've always wanted.
- I need you to add spice and meaning to my life.
- You make me feel like I'm needed.

- **My** husband and **I** need you to help make our lives complete.
- **I** need someone to love.

Sharing such things will help promote transparency in a child and build confidence with the knowledge that they are special.

Love Power

Love (true love) never fails. It leaves one genuinely desiring the betterment of another regardless of any personal pleasure or gain. It would probably surprise us to know the large number of people who live their entire lives without ever truly loving anyone but themselves.

Love longs to empower. It empowers by letting a person know that she is special. And as said earlier: You're only special if you're needed.

Foster children have an even greater need to be needed. Little things, such as, letting them know that it blesses you that they appreciate your cooking and that you actually need their compliments. This enables the child to feel valuable. The simple fact that you need something from them will make them feel special and boost their self esteem.

Isn't it ironic that instead of maximizing efforts to convince a person that they're needed, we sometimes go out of our way to prove the opposite. "I was doing well before you came along and I'll do just as well without you." Sound familiar? This is exactly what we should avoid communicating. People need to be needed. Of all the words that will ever enter one's ears, few are as empowering as: I need you. If our loved ones conclude that we do not need them, whether diligently or casually, they will seek someone who does.

Recently, I received a call from a young man (whom I will call **Mr. Carter**) who was having serious marital problems. He said it was urgent and he needed an appointment for counseling with me as soon as possible. His wife had given him a deadline to vacate the premises and refused to hear anything he had to say. The following day when he entered my office, I knew immediately that the situation was critical. We talked for a while, then I asked,

"Why is she so angry with you?"

"I made a mistake. She claims she can't forgive me."

"Love is able to forgive," I said. "Before this happened, did she love you?"

"Yes, I believe she did."

I then opened my Bible to the thirteenth chapter of First Corinthians and explained verses 4 through 8 as follows:

Love is slow to lose patience (it looks for a way of being constructive. It is not possessive: it is neither anxious to impress nor does it cherish inflated ideas of its own importance. Love has good manners and does not pursue selfish advantage. It is not touchy. It does not compile statistics of evil or gloat over the wickedness of other people. On the contrary, it is glad when truth prevails. Love knows no limit to its endurance, no end to its trust, no fading of its hope, it can outlast anything. It is, in fact, the one thing that still stands when all else has fallen. (Phillips)

"Is the issue that she truly believes she no longer loves you or has she convinced herself that you do not love her?"

"She's convinced I don't love her."

"Have you told her that you love her?"

"Yes, but she claims I'm lying."

"Have you told her recently that you need her?"

"Yes."

"Well, why don't you try telling her again, but this time do it in public, in front of your closest friends."

"OK, but I doubt if it'll make much difference."

Six days later I received a letter in a light pink envelope with the return address showing: The Carters. It was written by his wife, signed by both of them and mailed from San Diego, where they had gone to get away for a romantic weekend.

We should never underestimate the power of love, or the enormity of the need to be needed.

Six

No Regrets

*A*s a youngster **I** can remember asking my grandmother to tell me about our grandfather. She would only shake her head and walk away. Nothing about him was ever mentioned.

My grandmother was eighty-five years-old and living in **New York** when **I** received a call from her neighbor informing me that she was beginning to have difficulty getting around. Gramma was always a proud woman, intellectual and eloquent. **A** walking newspaper, she kept current on all social issues including health and politics. For the last twenty years she's grabbed every opportunity to tell anyone who would listen, how she worked until age seventy as a nurse in pediatrics.

Many years earlier, **I** prayed that if ever my grandmother's health diminished or she no longer wanted to live alone, that **God** would make it possible for her to come live with me. The following month, after getting approval from my wife, I flew to New York and moved Gramma to Los Angeles.

One day while we sat in the den reminiscing, I decided to try and impress upon Gramma the importance of breaking her silence regarding my grandfather. "You know you're eighty-five years old, Gramma, and though I hope you live to be one hundred and ten; at your age anything can happen. You've never said one word about our grandfather, and should you die, a significant part of our heritage goes with you.

"There's nothing to talk about," she insisted.

"Gramma, to deny my children the knowledge of their history simply because of pride would be a tragedy. You've always claimed you wanted the best for us; well, the best that you can give us is our history."

After about three hours of prodding, while crying profusely, she reluctantly conceded. "Forgive me," she pleaded. "I never meant to hurt any of you. I only tried to spare you my shame."

"These are different times, Gramma. Your story wouldn't even raise an eyebrow today."

Her sobbing gave testimony of how horrible it must have been to have a child out of wedlock back in 1929. And as she later revealed, for that child to be the fruit of a one night stand with a man who never loved her, was devastating.

"His name was John Thomas," she began. "I hadn't known him very long."

This she said so she wouldn't have to lie in the event

I should ask her if she loved him.

"I made a mistake. I thought he loved me, but he didn't." This she concluded from his failure to show up for their next date. Feeling used and unaware that she was pregnant, she distanced herself from him completely.

"What was he like?" I asked.

"He was a kind man, nice looking, dark skinned, neatly dressed. He seemed so much different than other men."

"How did he respond when he found out you were pregnant?"

"I saw no reason to tell him."

"Could he have found out from someone else?"

"No."

"Do you know if he's still living?"

"I don't know, I never saw him again. However, someone did tell me that they had heard he was living in Bedford Hills, New York."

"Was that recently?"

"Well, about six years ago."

"Then there's a chance he's still living! Gramma, I've got to find out."

Within three weeks, my wife and I were on a flight to New York in search of my grandfather. We arrived on Saturday evening, spent the night in a hotel in White Plains, then drove to Bedford Hills in the morning.

We arrived there just shortly after 10:00 a.m. It was a very small, quaint town just outside of Connecticut, where the pace of life was as I would have imagined it to be in the forties. Odds were that a black man who would enjoy such a snail-paced community would likely be the kind of man who would want to settle down; possibly go to church.

So, the church is where I decided to start my search. I figured that a longtime resident in his nineties would be easy to find in a town with a small black population and only a handful of black churches.

I tried to imagine my grandfather's personality and the kind of church he'd attend.

"There's a church!" my wife said, pointing to a life-less-looking building surrounded by overgrown shrubbery.

"I don't believe that's the one," I said. "It doesn't have my grandfather's personality." Knowing how unusually meticulous and proper my grandmother had always been, made it easy to visualize the kind of man she'd probably be attracted to.

Then suddenly, up ahead, as if supernaturally led, my eyes came to rest on a beautiful, white church, nestled at the foot of a hill and surrounded by towering oak trees. It was an older church, with a traditional style; strong looking and well-preserved. Totally captivated, I felt like Moses being drawn to a mysterious light.

"This is it!" I whispered excitedly to my wife. "I can sense it in my spirit."

We parked and walked up the path to the front of the church. The morning service had recently ended. A few people were standing outside, though most had already gone. As we approached the steps, a couple in their early forties were just coming out.

"Good morning," they greeted us, with a very pleasant smile. "Welcome to our church. Is this your first time here?" asked the husband.

"Yes, it is," I answered. "We've just arrived in town from California. I'm looking for my grandfather whom I've never met. I was told he lives here in Bedford Hills."

"Well, I've lived here all my life," he said. "What's his name?"

"John Thomas," I replied. "He should be in his nineties."

"Sure, we knew him well. Unfortunately, he died just eight months ago."

Suddenly, once again, there I was on that freeway with all the exits closed. I just couldn't believe it. Standing motionless with my mouth hanging open, I began to question God.

Why Lord? Why? You had thirty years in which to bring me here. Why would you let him die 8 months prior to my arrival? Instantly my mind recalled Romans chapter 8 verse 28:

And we know that all things work together for good to them that love God, to them who are the called according to His purpose.

"By the way, my name is Robert and this is my wife Angela."

"Hi, I'm Percival Dawson and this is my wife, Marie."

"How well did you know him?" I asked.

"Quite well," he responded. "He was married to my grandmother."

"What! John Thomas was your grandfather?"

"Remarkable, isn't it," he replied.

"Is your grandmother still living?"

"No, she died five years ago. Why don't you come home with us," he offered. "My mother would love to meet you and I'm sure you'll be interested in going through our photo albums."

I thought to myself, scenes like this only happen in the movies. After traveling three thousand miles looking for a man that I've never met, I enter a strange town and the first person I speak to is his grandson.

"It just so happens that we have a special program at church this afternoon," said Percival. "So if you come back with us I'll introduce you to Pastor Rufus Struther. He and John were very close. I'm sure he'll have a lot to share with you.

The Dawsons lived only a mile or so down the road. His mother was not at home. After eating, talking and browsing through photos, it was time to return to church. We decided to go a little early in hopes of meeting with the pastor.

The moment we entered the church, I said to myself, "This is exactly the kind of church I would want for myself." With a warm greeting the pastor welcomed us into his office. His eyes sparkled as Percival explained who I was.

"So you're Thomas' grandson, are you? I knew your grandfather for many years. He was a man that this town will not soon forget. Tell me, why did you wait until now to try and locate him?"

"I just found out who he was three weeks ago. My

grandmother broke her silence for the first time in 61 years." I then went on to explain why my grandmother was too ashamed to ever speak of him.

"Yeah, people back then didn't too much talk about those things," he said. "It's too bad 'cause he would have loved to have known you. Your grandfather was a kind, loving, God-fearing man. He came to this town just prior to the 1929 depression, and started a trash hauling business.

"When most of the town's businesses folded, your grandfather was one of the few people who continued to make money. Somebody always had a need to get rid of trash. As it turned out, your grandfather became the wealthiest black man in town and helped many of the townspeople refinance their businesses. As a matter of fact, John Thomas' money helped build this church."

I tried hard to maintain my same facial expression as my mind quickly recalled the many years of agony and disappointment experienced by my mother and her children. To think, we grew up as penniless orphans while our grandfather was supporting the dreams of his friends. Not to mention the fact that I was a struggling pastor who could only dream of a church as beautiful as this one. How I could have used his help!

"Did you talk to John's daughter, Claire Dawson or any of the other family members, Patricia or Danny?"

"Yes, I did talk to Claire. She shared a lot of information and showed me family pictures. I could clearly see the resemblance between John and my mother. I could also tell that he and his family were very close."

"Yes, John really loved his family," he said. "He treated those children like they were his own."

"You mean, they were not his biological children?"

"No, he was Alma's second husband. John died believing that he had no natural children."

"What! Then my mother was his sole heir?"

"Apparently so."

For a quick moment I found myself wanting to ask the Lord the same type of question which was asked by His disciples about the man who was born blind.

Who did sin, this man, or his parents, that he was born blind?

John 9:2

It would seem that someone did something very wrong to bring such bad luck upon my family. In my heart I knew that luck had nothing to do with it. I knew that the Lord would have given me the same answer that He gave His disciples:

Neither hath this man sinned, nor his parents: but that the works of God should be made manifest in him.

John 9:3

It was not the fornication which resulted in my mother's birth or the birth of her children that charted our course. It was the wisdom of God in mending that which was torn and straightening that which was crooked (all for His glory and the building of His Kingdom). My zeal to help disadvantaged, disenchanted people can be attributed largely to my past experiences. Who knows what I may have become had my mother continued to live. With her to encourage and direct me, I'm sure I would have been successful; but a pastor—doubtful.

"It's time for service to start," said Pastor Struther, glancing at his watch. "I'd like you to sit next to me on the platform." As we headed for the sanctuary, I found myself focusing on every detail of the building, almost as though I intended to purchase it. The plush carpet, the chandelier, the piped organ, and every beam in the ceiling bore witness of my grandfather's generosity which could have made life better for us.

I thought about my sister, Betty, now living in Los Angeles, and how childhood neglect and abuse affected her confidence and career. Though one of the most naturally gifted leaders I've known, she struggled for years with two children, Traci and Eddie, to get off welfare and she succeeded!

I thought about my brother, Maxie, presently living in Harlem, and the despicable lifestyle he had to adopt in order to survive. I thought about my brother, Freddie, whom I hadn't seen in 20 years. And then my sister, Doris, living in Oakland, California, whose four year old son was dying from AIDS which he contracted from her at birth. She had been infected years earlier by her boyfriend, a heroin addict. I often think, had we been raised together, living in the same home, I doubt if she would have gone in that direction.

The church was packed with members. After praying and singing a few hymns, Pastor Struther called me to the podium and introduced me to the congregation. When they learned who I was and why we were there, they went out of their way to show us love. One after another, people would come to me, give me a big hug and tell me how their views had changed after hearing of my experiences. Their love caused the scales to fall from my eyes, revealing God's wonderful plan for my life. It allowed me to see the bigger picture which encompassed far more than just me and my family. I felt really special. My heart was warmed and filled with love and that love left me with no regrets.

Love is the most powerful force on earth. It's the only thing that will enable a person to rejoice in the face of something regrettable. For certain people and in certain situations, money may cause them to look the other way. But ignoring pain is not the same as being delivered from it.

Hatred stirreth up strifes: but love covereth all sins.

Proverbs 10:12

In Genesis chapter 37, Joseph, the youngest and favorite son of Jacob, was sold into slavery by his brothers who hated him. They told their father that he had been killed by a wild beast. In trying to do what was right, Joseph ended up spending 13 years in prison for something he didn't do. I'm sure it was just as difficult for him to see God's hand in that situation as it was for me to perceive that God's hand was guiding me in mine. Once God intervened, Joseph was not only freed, but exalted to the second most powerful position in all of Egypt. The height of his joy was at the birth of his son, whom he named Manasseh, which means: He has made me "to forget."

Did he forget the hatred expressed by his brothers, the trip to Egypt as a slave, prison food, or the false charge of rape? No, those memories would be with him for the rest of his life. He was saying that his love for his son became a powerful distraction. A distraction so strong that it caused those painful experiences to become so insignificant that his mind declined to even deal with them.

It's not material possessions, not a position of power, but only love that can cause a person to forget 13 years of wrongful incarceration. At some point in time, everyone of us will likewise need a distraction to help us forget some unpleasant experience. The strongest distraction is love.

The first nine months of 1983 were the happiest months of my life. My wife and I were expecting our first child. Every aspect of the birthing process fascinated me. From the first sound of his muffled heart beat through a stethoscope, to his first resounding wail, I was intent on every detail. Seemed like God was finally making-up for my many years of disappointment (little did I know that there was yet more to be learned).

Once out of the womb, I noticed a rather large hole at the base of our son's back. A previous ultrasound test had revealed enlarged ventricles, prompting doctors to alert a specialist. He was rushed to surgery to seal the opening (a defect known as spina bifida).

Six days later, a tube (called a shunt) was placed in

his head to relieve blockage of the spinal fluid. We were told, prior to surgery, that our son probably would not walk or stand without braces; may not have normal mental functions; may not have normal sensory reception in his hands and in other extremities; and, would likely require hundreds of thousands of dollars in medical bills.

Being a minister of the gospel of Jesus Christ and knowing the healing power of God, my confidence never wavered that all would turn out well. Many people have said to me, had it been their child they would not have been able to handle it. They marveled as though I was some exceptionally strong individual.

However, my only advantage was that I truly believed God loved me. I love the Lord and I love my son, and that love makes it impossible for me to regret any experience involving either one of them. *Webster* defines "regret" as: *Sorrow aroused by circumstances beyond one's power to control or remedy.* It's a feeling that follows a painful or distressing experience (an event that one would certainly want to avoid repeating). To regret is to be sorrowful.

"Sorrow" is defined as: *Uneasiness or anguish due to loss (as of something loved or familiar); a cause of grief or sadness.* Sorrow is an emotion. Emotions tend to cloud issues and get in the way of good judgment.

Love is the only force strong enough to restrain our emotions, enabling us to get beyond initial feelings and deal rationally with the truth. And yes, my son's medical bills did exceed **$200,000** in the first **18** months and I slept many nights curled up on those little hospital convertible chairs. But if you saw our son today, you would not be able to detect any disability, though there are a number of problems he has yet to overcome.

Now, of course, our experience is not one that I would have intentionally ordered for me or anyone else, but if faced, once again, with the same situation, I'd make no attempt to avoid repeating it.

Just a year and a half after our son was born, my wife and I were challenged with another heart wrenching situation. My wife had always wanted a little girl. After a misread ultrasound test, she was mistakenly told that her first pregnancy was a girl. It took her weeks to recover from that error. Eight months later she was pregnant again. An amniocentesis confirmed a baby girl. Once again she was back on cloud nine.

In the latter part of the fifth month, my wife developed a bad cough and shortly thereafter her water bag broke. We rushed to the hospital and were told that her vital signs were such that the pregnancy would have to be terminated. Otherwise, they could give only a 50/50 chance that my wife would survive the next 24 hours.

"Can the baby be removed by cesarean section," I asked.

"No, she would need to remain intact a little longer to insure development sufficient to breathe on her own."

"I'll be alright!" my wife insisted.

The doctor motioned for me to step outside the room. "I know how much this baby means to your wife, but she must consider seriously the risk involved. There is a strong possibility we could lose her."

I wondered why the Lord would confront me with a test that exactly paralleled what happened to my mother. She went to the hospital with pregnancy complications and never came back home.

The flashback had an affect on my faith. I just couldn't take the risk. I went back and convinced my wife that the risk was too great—we had to induce labor.

Assuming that I understood how it feels for a woman to lose a child was a major mistake. For weeks my wife would stay in bed with the covers pulled over her head. It took the counseling of two very wise and sensitive women to help her understand how much God and I both loved her and that she should love herself just as much as before losing the baby. Two years later, we had another son. And four years after his birth, we had our daughter.

Truth

In the same month that my wife became pregnant with Ryan, our first son, I fractured my hip in a freak accident on the basketball court. It took over seven months to recuperate. In addition to having to endure the most excruciating pain I've ever felt, my doctor alerted me that I could possibly end up walking with a limp. Thank God that didn't happen. In spite of the pain, the entire ordeal turned out to be a marvelous blessing. In fact, it was my memory of that pain which cushioned the news about my son.

Like many expecting parents, I would find myself contemplating what positive genetic traits and characteristics would likely pass on to my son. Being a distance runner, I looked forward to running with my son, expecting to have provided him with a great pair of legs and strong lungs.

Ironically, it was the fractured hip experience that became my cushion for the word *spina bifida*, making it easy to relate to his condition. I could see and enjoy the person that he is, not the character I selfishly desired him to be. As Ryan grew older, it became apparent to me that my fractured hip experience had sufficiently prepared me for his disability. Likewise, the problems borne out of my foster care experience furnished me with the necessary sensitivity and insight to anticipate and respond appropriately to his needs.

Shortly after Ryan turned ten years old, I noticed him starting to lie habitually. Like a swerving drunk driver, it grabbed my attention. Without help, I knew he would crash against the barricades in his mind (the same type of barricades which I too had erected, and mine hadn't too long ago been torn down). Many foster children and most who are disabled, wrestle with feelings of inferiority. Of all the problems that I longed to overcome, the one I despised the most was lying.

For me, lying was bondage. I wanted to be normal like everybody else. I hated having to explain why I lived where I did; what happened to my mother; why I could not have company over, etc. As soon as I would tell one group of friends, invariably I would move again and have to start all over. Before long, I would lie just to avoid conversation.

I'd lie about my past, lie about the present, sometimes I would even lie about my name. I didn't lie to
manipulate people or gain power over them. I lied to gain
acceptance, to avoid embarrassment, to escape the bonds
of inferiority and capture a moment of normalcy. Every
time I had to lie, I felt like a saddled mule on a range
with wild horses. Everyone was free but me.

The freest, most enviable person in town is the one
who does not have to resort to lying about anything to
anyone. To lie means that you have not yet excelled to a
level where it's no longer necessary to insult your integrity
and compromise your character to remain in the good
graces of another. Thank God I've been delivered. I've
learned that I don't have to lie. God's word says I'm
special and I believe it. Therefore, lying is an option that
I refuse to choose.

*All things are lawful unto me, but all things are
not expedient: all things are lawful for me, but I will
not be brought under the power of any.*

I Corinthians 6:12

I know this sounds ridiculous. We live in a society
that not only models and encourages lying, but estab-
lishes mindless regulations that make it almost impossible
for some people to avoid doing so. Refusing to do so sig-
nifies conviction and respect for yourself. In addition to
exercising courage and confidence, it can be an imposing
expression of power.

How excellent is the marriage of good character and
integrity—two things that a liar does not have. Refusing to

lie is one of the greatest expressions of love and respect for
oneself. Position, power, achievements and wealth will
always command certain respect. But how can I esteem a
person who cannot (by God's standards) esteem himself?

*Nothing heralds the fact that you have not yet
arrived, as having to lie to get by.*

Robert Colwell

I could never admire a liar. Ryan's reason for lying
was obvious. I felt I could help him, but I needed the
right opening. One day as I picked him up from school,
I noticed he had been crying. When he told me why (leaving out a few important details) I knew it was the perfect
time. You see, Ryan had a problem—he could never admit when he was wrong or that someone else was better
than he.

Here's what happened. One of Ryan's classmates (a
girl) challenged him to a race. "I bet I can run faster than
you, Ryan."

"No you can't," he replied.

Not only did she win the race, but came back and
teased him in front of everyone on the playground. I had
seen the same thing happen many times at home. One
day all three kids were bouncing on our bed turning flips.
Justin, who is three years younger than Ryan, did a perfect flip. Chelsea, who is seven years younger, did a perfect flip also. But when Ryan tried, his head started hurting so much, he had to stop.

Typical of a five year old, Chelsea challenged him

saying that she could do it better. Ryan, of course, had to prove her wrong. A few minutes later, I found him stretched out on his bed crying. Once again, a girl had beaten him.

I decided to wait until just before dinner to discuss what had happened at school. I took him alone into the living room, sat down on the sofa and started sharing with him.

"For the most part Ryan," I started, "what adults say and do in the presence of others depend a lot on what they think the other person's response will be. Will they walk away, get angry, challenge, get excited, cry, quit, or show appreciation?

"Kids, on the other hand, don't usually take the time to think about how their words or actions will affect another. They love to outdo one another. It's difficult for kids to refuse a challenge or walk away from an opportunity to prove that they are the best. Adults sometimes act like children when it comes down to reacting to something said or done to them. They may blurt out the first thing that comes to mind without giving it a thought. All of us have done it, and that may be what you did today. Let's talk about what happened today."

After going back over the story, I said, "Your feelings got hurt because you reacted to a challenge without thinking about how it would turn out. I used to do that too. As a matter of fact, you're doing exactly what I did—lying to keep from looking bad."

His eyes widened. "That's right, I used to lie to make myself look good, because I saw myself as inferior. And now you're doing it. You knew you couldn't outrun that girl, but you couldn't bring yourself to admit it. God knew what He was doing when He told us not to lie. It's the truth that makes us free. A weakling will always lie to avoid embarrassment, but a strong person will try and tell the truth. I was weak until made strong by God.

"You'll find that the kids will stop teasing you, will respect you and even include you more, when they find out the truth. So, the next time anyone comes up to you and challenges you to a race, look them right in the eyes and say: 'I was born with a birth defect that damaged my spine, and because of it, I cannot run as fast as you.'"

Water filled his eyes. "Do you think you can say that with me, Ryan?"

Choked up and sobbing, he answered, "Yes."

"Ok, repeat this after me."

"I was born,"

"I was b-b-born," he was so upset, he could barely speak,

"with a birth defect,"

"w-w-with a a birth d-def-fect,"

"that damaged my spine,"

"that d-damaged my my spine."

When we finished he was still crying, so I walked him through it again. I told him that I wanted him to continue saying it until he could say it boldly with confidence.

The seventh time through it, I could see in his face that he had finally gotten comfortable with it. The eighth time through, I was confident that it had gotten down into his spirit. I gave him a big hug. And as I hugged him, I thanked God for the way that He had brought me, for the things that He had taught me, for the wisdom to help my son, and for an understanding of the power of a hug.

Things seemed to really improve. The lying stopped and Ryan appeared to have more confidence. One day I was at the kitchen table studying, when I heard Ryan yelling hysterically. I got up to see what was wrong and found him stretched out on his bed wailing bitterly. The other kids were with my wife, Angela, in our bedroom sitting on our bed.

"What's going on?" I asked.

Justin answered, "Ryan is mad because Mommy gave me this toothbrush and he wants it."

"You mean, he's crying like that over a toothbrush?"

"Yes."

I called for Ryan to come to our room. I had never seen him so hysterical.

"What's this all about, Ryan?" I had to repeat myself twice before he could compose himself enough to answer.

"The toothbrush belonged to me!" he sobbed. My wife was silent, so I knew she had to be involved.

"Ok, Angela, does the toothbrush belong to Ryan?"

"No, here's the story. I saw some pretty, designer toothbrushes in a specialty shop and decided to get one. When I realized they were on sale, I picked up an extra. When I got home Ryan asked me who the other toothbrush was for and I told him it's for whoever needs it.

He then asked if he could have it, but the one he has is nearly new. A couple of days later, Justin asked if I would buy him a new toothbrush because his was worn out. He showed it to me, and it was old and frayed, so I gave the new toothbrush to him."

Looking at Ryan I asked, "Is that the way it happened?" He nodded his head, yes. So I said, "Tell me, Ryan, would you agree that all people should strive to always make wise decisions?"

"Yes."

"Would you also agree that being wise is better than being foolish?"

"Yes."

"Well, answer this for me. Let's say you are a father. You have two children and only one new toothbrush which both of them want. One child's toothbrush is nearly new, the other's is old and worn out. What do you think is the wiser thing to do? Give it to the child whose toothbrush is new, and make the other child use his old one until the next time you go to the store? Or, give it to the one whose toothbrush is old, and the next time you are at the store, pick up another one for the other child?" He just stood there looking at me with tears in his eyes.

"C'mon, Ryan, who would you give it to?"

After another long pause he answered, "I don't know."

I knew then we really needed to talk. "Well, Ryan, let's go in your room so we can discuss this further." Dragging his feet, he followed me. We sat on the edge of his bed.

"Ryan, you're my son and I love you; and I also know how smart you are. You agreed that a person should always strive to make wise decisions, and I am sure you realize that your answer was not wise. What I don't know is why you said that you don't know who the toothbrush should go to. I need you to tell me."

His response blew me away. In over eighteen years of counseling hundreds of people, rarely have I heard an answer as mature and candid as his.

"Justin," he said, "gets everything that he wants. He's the one that's so popular. He's the one that everybody calls cute. He's the one that can outrun everybody and wins all the basketball games and has all the friends. He's everything that I want to be, and I don't want him to have my toothbrush!"

I paused a moment and then said, "Ryan, that was a very mature response you just gave me. I'm really impressed. I know a lot of adults who could never admit that. I'm going to share something with you and I don't want you to ever forget it.

"With every emotional issue there is the truth, and the way you feel about it. Never let the way you feel about it get in the way of the truth. Now, the way you feel about it is, of course, very important. So, whenever it's wise to express your feelings, you should always try and do so. But your feelings should not stand in front of the truth.

"The proper response to my question should have been: I know that the toothbrush should go to Justin, but I don't want him to have it. With that answer, I would have opportunity to ask you why not, and then take into consideration your answer."

I then called Justin to come into the room. He pushed open the door immediately, which let me know that he had been standing there listening the whole time.

"Justin, I want you to give Ryan the toothbrush." Having heard what Ryan said about him, I could see in his face a longing for Ryan to have it. His response warmed my heart. I then said to Ryan, "It's not because you deserve it, nor that Justin was wrong that you are getting the toothbrush. It's only because, when I considered the circumstances and the effect it may have on each of you, I concluded that you both will be better served if I let you have it."

As I left the room, I heard Justin ask Ryan if he wanted to play a video game with him.

Expectations

By being raised in foster homes, I was unaccustomed to birthdays being a big celebration. Little attention was given to it; therefore, to me it was just another day. My wife, on the other hand, comes from a family who treats birthdays as a major event.

Consequently, each year she would try and plan something big for my birthday, but I repeatedly rejected her ideas, choosing rather to simply stay at home and enjoy pound cake with strawberries and whipped cream. Having no interest in celebrating my own birthday I saw little reason to get excited about hers, in spite of her efforts to convince me otherwise. It wasn't that I lacked interest or a desire to see her happy, I just lacked motivation.

One day while counseling a woman whose husband was just like me, the eyes of my understanding opened as she broke down in tears, telling me how she was devastated by her husband's refusal to celebrate her birthday. Her husband had disappointed her four years in a row. Talk about being convicted. My wife and I had been married 10 years and each of her birthdays was disappointing.

In light of this, I decided to make my wife's next birthday a very special event. I invited her friends and all the staff at our church to a surprise birthday party at our home. I ordered her favorite cake (made from scratch, enough to feed 40 people) and bought her a new pair of shoes and a purse. I instructed the guests to arrive promptly between 8:50 and 9:00 p.m. On the morning of her birthday she arose with the same cheerfulness that she always starts her birthday with.

"Happy birthday", I said casually, which gave clear indication that my attitude had not changed. All day long she heard nothing from me. No phone calls to her job, no flowers, no candy.

After an unremarkable dinner, I pulled from the refrigerator a frozen, Sara Lee pound cake, had the kids put some candles in it and served it with vanilla ice cream. With every bite she took she would bristle.

"Thank you, that was delicious," she said. Then announced that she was tired and went up to bed.

Was she angry, or was she angry! Her inability to change my attitude left her feeling powerless and full of emotions which caused her to ignore some very clear signs that something was going on.

First of all, in general, she knows me to be a very thoughtful and generous person. She knows I would not have insulted her by serving frozen pound cake, knowing I had failed to get her a gift. Secondly, it took me and the children (whose ages at the time were nine, seven and two) over an hour to straighten up the house and hang all the decorations. All the while, the door to the dining room was closed (which rarely is) and none of the children were playing or watching television.

And when has she ever known me to vacuum the living room and dining room after **8:00** at night? Most significant was the fact that we have a large German Shepherd dog who goes crazy every time someone comes near our house. If someone comes up on the porch he slams against the gate which can be heard from anywhere in the house.

All the guests were told not to ring the doorbell, but to knock lightly. A number of them arrived early and were standing in front of the house waiting for others. At **8:50** the first group tapped on the door. The dog went crazy. "Rarr, rarr, rarr, rarr." I opened the door and directed them into the living room.

A few minutes later, "Rarr, rarr, rarr, rarr," and more guests came in. About eight times I answered the door and each time the dog went crazy. Now, knowing full well that the dog only acts like that when someone is at the door, she totally ignored the signs because she did not expect anyone to come by.

Unless you expect to see a thing, it can easily be overlooked. In the book of Matthew chapter 9, beginning at verse 20:

A lot of people in the crowd were touching Jesus, but only the woman with the issue of blood had an expectation of being healed upon touching him. Therefore, she was the only one that was healed.

Only a touch filled with faith could command the attention of Jesus. It's not enough just to touch a person, but you must touch them in the way they long to be touched in order to receive all that they are capable of giving you.

At 9:05 p.m. I called for my wife to come into the living room.

"I'm tired, I don't feel like getting up," she responded. After five minutes of prodding she came through the door. By her bedroom appearance it was obvious she had no expectation of seeing anyone. As the room filled with the shouts of, "Happy Birthday," in a moment, she was magically hoisted from her pit of powerlessness, empowered by the knowledge that I loved her enough to change and to show her and her friends that she was special.

Watching her was quite an experience—one I didn't expect. It was as though she was six years old again. All it took was one hour of loving, unselfish attention. It left her with no regrets and released me from a ten year old debt.

Heart of Love

When my mother died, it was as though my mind shut down. I couldn't concentrate on anything. Life became one great big distraction. I never did any homework, rarely ever turned in work assignments or studied for any test. I relied totally on what I picked up in the classroom. Consequently, when I graduated from high school, my comprehension of the English language was so poor (in my opinion) that I was afraid to write a letter, or send a postcard to anyone. I believed my writing was inferior to everyone else's and I feared looking like a moron.

Writing this book is an attempt to break free from the yoke that has held me in bondage most of my life. I realize that this book is not a "literary work of art." But I'm awed each time I flip through the pages and reflect on the fact that I wrote every word. Hallelujah!

Previously, I mentioned briefly that at age eleven when my mother died, I put down my baritone horn and never picked it up again. At age 38, while sitting at my kitchen table, finalizing my Sunday morning sermon, I thought of how a good song directly related to what I intended to say would help drive home my message.

Suddenly, words started popping up in my head. Within one hour I had written all the words to the song. I then started thinking of a tune. I sat down at my wife's piano and with one finger, pecked out a tune in just 20 minutes. I telephoned my extremely gifted former church pianist, Sharon John, and asked her to stop by my house on the way to church. She rushed over, pulled out a music sheet and charted the chords as I sang her the tune. We both felt the song was a hit.

When we sang it at church, the congregation loved it so much that I proposed to write another. By the end of that year, I had written an entire album, and another album the following year. My wife suggested I enter the Billboard song writer's contest. I submitted four songs and received awards for two of them, which were the last song and the very first one.

I've often wondered what life may have been like for me had someone taken the time to check with my elementary school teachers to determine my interests. Perhaps after learning that I was musically gifted, they would have encourage me to pursue a career in music, instead of Food Trades and Machine Shop. Maybe I would have been another Quincy Jones or Henry Mancini.

Maybe my sister, Betty, who presently works for the phone company and is a part-time travel agent, would be the CEO of a major corporation. It bothers me when I think of the fact that she is probably a more skillful, tenacious and outgoing business and people person, than most of the bosses she's had to work under.

Maybe my sister, Doris, who is HIV positive, would still have her health. Having worked as a legal secretary, she currently works for an organization of activists for all disabled persons. She has traveled to many cities speaking on disability and particularly AIDS related issues. In 1992, she was sent to Germany for the annual conference on **AIDS** to speak on a panel representing black women affected by **AIDS**. She has also appeared on a number of television talk shows. She and her husband, **R**oderick, are strong Christians, working faithfully in their church.

Maybe my brother, Freddie, would not have spent 20 years in the **N**avy, which he did not always enjoy, but was concerned about his future had he left. **M**aybe my brother, **R**aymond, would be a television producer. He's worked for the same company as a chauffeur for over 15 years and is now a part-time office maintenance manager. **F**or the past 5 years, he's produced a weekly gospel talk show on cable television. **T**hough he did have a short bout with alcohol and drugs, he is now a solid Christian and is the sound technician at his church.

And maybe my brother, **M**axie, who presently works as a waiter in a posh **N**ew **Y**ork **C**ity restaurant, would at least have some idea of his potential. **A**s a young child, he appeared to have more "star" qualities than the rest of us. But with numerous negative experiences and no support, he has truly suffered as a victim of the system.

He became a drug user, a thief, a con artist and a male whore. **H**e was homeless, sleeping on subway trains at night and panhandling in **G**rand **C**entral **S**tation during the day. **H**e is now a member of the outreach team at his church, reaching out to the homeless and the hard core street people of lower **M**anhattan.

I guess, in many ways, we've all suffered. **A**djusting to different homes can be difficult. **E**ach foster parent has different standards and methods of doing things. **S**ometimes the child is required to adjust to the very thing that the previous parent condemned. Who knows if we'll ever fully comprehend the impact of multiple placements. This is why, in my training sessions to foster parents and potential foster parents, I stress the importance of commitment in the decision to take in a child.

Looking over the past, if left up to me, there are many things I would loved to have changed, many experiences I would have avoided. But God has used every experience to help me understand and demonstrate His love and His love has left me with no regrets.

So, when I'm speaking to welfare, foster or adoption agencies, teens in schools, inmates, married couples, church members, the disability community, or others, it's God's love that empowers and shines through me. His love, through Christ, is the greatest gift that He could ever give.

I can't change my childhood, but I can influence and empower my kids. I can teach them through my experiences and through God's word, to love and respect themselves, as well as other people, and to cherish and depend on God's love. His love will teach them how to love, and prepare their hearts to make right choices.

One of the things I am most proud of, is that I have successfully convinced my children that I have no regrets for marrying their mother, and that they can always depend on me to respect and support her. I want them to understand that in all that they do, if they love themselves and the God who made them, they will have no regrets for what is done from the heart.

Of all that is worthy of our best efforts to hold on to, the last thing any of us can afford to lose is hope.